& LIFE GOES ON...

Major Thomas
2019

Major Thomas

& Life Goes On...

Copyright © 2019 by Major Thomas

All rights reserved. No part of this book may be reproduced in any form or by any electronic or mechanical means, including information or retrieval systems, without permission in writing from the publisher, except by a reviewer who may quote brief passages in review.

Although the author and publisher have made every effort to ensure that the information in this book was correct at the time of publication, the author and publisher do not assume and hereby disclaim any liability to any party for loss, damage or disruption caused by errors or omissions, whether such errors or omissions result from negligence, accident or any other cause. This work contains the author's the author's subjective thoughts, ideas and opinion and memories. Individual names and situations may be altered to protect the privacy of those involved.

Printed in the United States of America

ISBN: 978 1794251700

FORWARD

My name is Major Thomas. I was born in St. Louis, Missouri on April, 24th, 1934. I lived a very comfortable life, from birth to present day. I lived through the end of the depression, during World War II and beyond.

I very vividly remember early years, victory gardens, rationing of important items needed for the war effort like: some foods, gasoline and tires. We listened to the radio about the war. I listened to the monotone, somber voices of reporters like Edward R. Morrow and Walter Cronkite. I heard the stories about General George Patton's progress on some of his marches.

I wondered how the people lived through all of the war's destruction and about the thousands of people killed. I heard of stories of Japanese torture from people who were stationed there.

Many of our glorious battleships were sunk and there was terrible destruction of airplanes and buildings. I heard reporters talk about the bombing of Pearl Harbor as they gave the statistics of wounded and killed service members.

The civilian population went to work building airplanes, tanks, special vehicles like jeeps, personnel carriers, even gas masks. Civilians helped to provide food for our troops. They manufactured tons and tons of ammunition. The list goes on and on. The general population rarely complained about the sacrifices made for the war effort.

During the invasion at Normandy, I was so intent on listening about the many thousands of our military dying for country. It was devastating and hard to understand how humanity could destroy itself.

Then came VE Day (Victory in Europe Day): the end of the war in Europe. When news of the Holocaust came, I thought of the many millions of people who lost their lives.

After VJ Day (Victory in Japan Day), war in the Pacific theater ended and life went on. Thousands of soldiers and other military personnel returned home to get their lives back together. Making babies by the thousands. Rationing was gone, new automobiles, auto parts, new tires and thousands of babies were made! Without rationing, gasoline, sugar, and other foods were plentiful again.

The G I bill helped our veterans get jobs, go to college and buy homes. I built my first home and went to truck driving school with the G I Bill after my service in the Korean War.

Then came the threat of invasion of South Korea by the North Koreans and China, in June, 1950.

I graduated from a small-town high school in 1952. A month or so after graduation, a very good friend and high school buddy came to visit me at home. We talked for quite a while, laying down on the beautiful grass, so green, with the air so fresh around us at my family's farm. What an enjoyable day.

We discussed the war going on in Korea. Both of us decided we should join the military. My father, served in the U.S. Navy from 1928 through 1932. So I had no problem with wanting to serve in the Navy. When I told my dad my plans, he said we would go see the recruiter the next Tuesday.

Then in mid-July, my friend and I went to St. Louis, Federal Building for a physical, indoctrination, some written tests and to be sworn in. I raised my right hand, and took the oath. That was the beginning of a totally different life style, a dramatic change for my future. This is the story of what made me who I am.

Major Thomas
Author

& Life Goes On...

Table of Contents

Chapter One: My Early Life 1
Chapter Two: Life in Owensville, Missouri 18
Chapter Three: High School 36
Chapter Four: Ahoy! Going to the Navy 41
Chapter Five: The LST's 48
Chapter Six: Navy Life 57
Chapter Seven: The Trip to Korea 64
Chapter Eight: War Zone: Korea 72
Chapter Nine: Operation Big Switch & War Stories ... 81
Chapter Ten: Liberty 95
Chapter Eleven: Duty Keeps Calling 101
Chapter Twelve: The War Ends? 107
Chapter Thirteen: Mrs. Sullivan 115
Chapter Fourteen: Navy Records 122
Chapter Fifteen: Back to Civilian Life 138
Chapter Sixteen: Erna and Me 140

& Life Goes On…

Table of Contents (cont.)

Chapter Seventeen: Our Family ………………………… 150

Chapter Eighteen: Work Life ………………………… 166

Chapter Nineteen: My Adoption ………………………… 174

Chapter Twenty: Good Times! ………………………… 178

Chapter Twenty One: Erna's Last Days on Earth………… 185

Chapter Twenty Two: My Life Without Erna …………… 190

Chapter Twenty Three: Picking Up the Pieces …………… 194

Chapter Twenty Four: The Honor Flight ………………… 199

Chapter Twenty Five: Life in Owensville These Days …… 205

Chapter Twenty Six: My Daughter Pam ………………… 214

Chapter Twenty Seven: Health and Happiness …………… 220

Chapter Twenty Eight: Final Thoughts …………………… 227

Major Thomas

Major Fred Thomas, Jr.
Born: April 24, 1934

St. Ann's Orphanage
St. Louis, Missouri

Birth Name:
John Leo Walde

Adopted by:
Major F. and Eva L. Thomas
1936

Chapter One:

My Early Life

My earliest childhood memories were of riding a tricycle in a flat at 920 S. Taylor Avenue in St. Louis, Missouri. I might have been three or four years of age. I played with some kids that I think were a couple of years older than me in the rear of the same flat.

Dad worked at Swift and Co. seventeen years as a yard supervisor. He worked in the yards with the cattle, hogs and sheep that came in from all over the state and other areas close around. He loved the work because he had his chance to be around livestock. Dad was raised a farm boy.

Major
920 South Taylor
Avenue

One day, Dad came home and said there was a terrible accident on the expressway, called a super highway. We lived about two flats away from the overpass so he could see it good. He told Mom trucks were involved. They would not allow trucks on the expressway after that.

We moved from the flat to 7720 W. Rankin in Richmond Heights, Missouri. I can still remember the phone number: HI (Highland) 3014.

In Richmond Heights I was very sick. I was in a bedroom that was very dimly lit. Mom came in to check on me. I have no idea what may have been the problem, but it wasn't normal lighting or normal activities.

7720 W. Rankin Place

& Life Goes On...

**First Known Picture of John L. Walde
Aka: Major F. Thomas, Jr.
Age is Unknow**

There was a picture on the top of a chest of drawers in the living room. One day I asked Mom who the cute little girl was because the person in the picture had very long curly blond hair. Mom said it was me. I couldn't believe it! I still have that picture. I am not sure how old I was when it was taken. I was wearing a sun suit, so perhaps around eighteen months to two years old. That's the first baby picture of me.

Mrs. Burns was a neighbor up the street from us. She would babysit for us. One evening Dad and Mom went out so Mrs. Burns came to be with us. I kept climbing the front yard fence, showing off. Mrs. Burns kept saying, "stay off the fence!" I fell and landed on my private parts, skinning my inner thighs. I told her I was alright, then went inside to bed. I hurt very, very bad. Mrs. Burns told Mom and Dad about it. The next morning, I got a good lecture from Dad and Mom.

Major Thomas

I hated, well, I was extremely afraid of black and white police cars. I'd either dreamed of something or something happened to me to give me this fear. But I remember a police car stopping in the front of the house. An officer got out and came around the back of the car. He opened the trunk and took something out, then came to the sidewalk where I was standing and bent over me. For some strange reason, I cannot forget this. It was very real to me. Since then, I have had a dreadful fear of the black and white police cars. Not so much in later years, as when I was very young.

During the Christmas season, Mom would bundle us up. We would get on a city bus and ride to Eighth and Olive or Tenth and Delmar. Right to the very center of downtown St. Louis. We would go see the window dressings. There were animations of life-size people, very interesting trains, animations of reindeer and other cute animals. We could watch them for hours on end.

It was extremely cold. I certainly enjoyed seeing all these neat things before Christmas day. I know we did that more than just once. The main attractions were the windows of Famous Barr and Stix Bear and Fuller. I am sure there were more.

Marbles was a fun game to play. I spent many hours shooting marbles on a playground, vacant lots, anywhere there was a little flat space.

We would draw a circle in the dust or dirt. Usually the circle would be about two feet in diameter. Each player would put up to six marbles in the center of the circle. There can be more than two players. Most players placed the marbles using a little strategy, hoping to make it harder for the rival players to pick an easy target. The object of the game was to go home with more marbles than when you started.

The shooter was special and was considered the most important part of playing marbles. Every shooter had his own technique on how to shoot. The shooter marble was a little larger than the regular marbles were. I tried to put some type of spin on the shooter marble to hit the target marble.

The goal was to knock the target marble out of the circle. When the shooter knocks a target marble to the outside of the circle, then that marble belongs to the shooter.

Sometimes the players would get a little feisty with each other, even a little fighting would break out. But never to the point where anyone was injured, just enough to vent frustrations.

I used to play in the wooded areas surrounding our house in Richmond Heights. We had a neat tire swing that was on a high tree limb. It could swing out for a good distance. Tommy O'hara and I would spend hours playing in the woods.

Dad would take me to work with him once a while at the Swift and Co. St. Louis stockyard located at Vandeventer and Chouteau streets. Sheep will not be driven or forced to go where you want them, so the stockyards had two "judas goats" the sheep would follow. When they wanted the sheep moved, especially to the killing floor, they would get the goats. Then let them mill around with the sheep. When they would open the gates, the sheep would follow them to the killing floor.

I went to the "killing floor" once, and was shocked with what I saw. The cows would be hit in the head with a big hammer, fall like a rock, put chains around legs and lift the cows up. The stockyard workers would "bleed" them by sticking a knife in their throat so the blood would gush out. I saw "floor killers" grab a cup, get a cup of blood and drink it. That almost made me sick to see.

Major Thomas

The old 'Dinky' streetcar, served Maplewood, Richmond Heights and Brentwood during the day. We got to know the old gentleman conductor. He would give us free rides from Bredell to the end of the line in Brentwood, if we changed the trolley.

*Major,
Little Flower School*

When we got to the end, he would take his changer and a special kind of "tool" that was used to turn a switch to make it move. We would go out and pull the trolley down, secure it under the holder, then go to the other end and raise the trolley. It had a type of carbon wheel that rode on the electrical cable.

At night we would go out while the conductor was stopped and pull the trolley down. All the lights would go out and the conductor would cuss, get out and try to get the trolley back on the cable so he could go again. It wasn't the same conductor we were pals with during the daytime.

I remember World War II very graphically. News commentators, like Edward R. Murrow, had very deep monotone voices. When they delivered the news about the "Battle of the Bulge", it sounded so graphic and intense that it scared me. I had dreams about it.

Mrs. Stuecks, a neighbor across the street in Richmond Heights, had three sons in the service. They were quite a bit older than me so never knew them. Mrs. Stuecks had a banner with stars on it hanging in her front room window. It represented the number of family members in the Armed Forces. She talked to mom a lot about her sons.

We planted victory gardens to help raise some of our own food. Gasoline rationing was serious. Dad would get extra ration stamps from some of the truckers who came in at Swift. The drivers were allowed enough ration stamps to cover the driving they had to do to get farm products to market.

Many people had to park their cars. They didn't have ration stamps, couldn't get tires, or they couldn't get the parts to keep their cars running. Dad bought a new bicycle to ride to work to save gas. I think he did it a day or two and that was the end of it. He gave the bike to me. He just didn't have the stamina.

Some foods like sugar, were much missed items. Then someone had the bright idea to substitute butter with what they called "oleo". Whatever this "oleo" was, you mixed coloring in it to make it look like butter. But it sure didn't taste like butter.

The radio was a very interesting home luxury. I would sit in front of it listening to programs like: Superman, Gang Busters, Terry and the Pirates, Fiber McGee and Molly, Amos and Andy, The Squeaking Door and many others.

But the news was most profound for me. I wondered how it must have been at some of the places the news commentator was talking about. Franklin D Roosevelt gave a speech about the bombing of Pearl Harbor: "A Day which will live in Infamy". Franklin D. Roosevelt spoke the truth.

The end of World War II, VJ Day, was a memorable day. Dad loaded us in the car and drove towards the downtown area. Cars were everywhere. Some cars were dragging 55 gallon barrels behind them, some honked their horns, and others flashed their lights. People were sticking their heads out of the windows and yelling. After V-J Day, there were no more Victory Gardens, no more gasoline or food rationing and new tires could be purchased again.

I thought the new Ford pickup trucks, (1947/1948), were the neatest looking vehicle I had ever seen. It was a very modern looking machine. New cars, new body styles were starting to appear.

During this time, my little sister Marilyn was born on January 11, 1941. Marilyn was Dad's pride and joy. Since my parents had two other boys and me, Dad had wanted a girl. And, he got one!

On January 11th, Dad went coon hunting in the early morning hours. The coon dog treed an animal in a fallen rotten log. Dad bent over to see if the coon was in there. Well, it wasn't a coon.

It was a skunk! Dad got 'perfumed' by the skunk. So, he couldn't come to the hospital because he smelled so bad. He had to wait to see his new baby daughter until the next day.

I rode my bicycle everywhere. Once in a while my friend and neighbor, Mike Farris, would ride on the handlebars. Mike didn't have a bike. One time when Mike was riding with me, the front tire hit a sewer drain grate, the tire wedged in the grate bars, stopping immediately. Mike was thrown off the bike and I was thrown down on the concrete street. I really injured my knee and still have a scar from that accident. Mike didn't get hurt too bad, but we were both pretty shook up.

There was a walking bridge over a large storm drainage canal/storm sewer in Maplewood. We liked to ride our bikes on it, then to the sidewalk, which was perpendicular to the bridge walk. If we were ornery or just lazy we would cut across this man's yard. He would raise hell with us. One time he got so mad, he cursed and threw a bucket at us. It didn't hit anyone, but we all remembered how angry he got so we steered clear of him for a while.

& Life Goes On...

Dad's friend Larry Horine, was a Richmond Heights police officer. Mr. Horine had two sons; who were a couple of years older than me. Sometimes we would go to Larry's dad's farm out in the country.

Once when we were walking in fields, we had to cross over a barbed-wire fence. After getting over the fence, I felt something different on my right elbow; I looked down and saw a deep gash. I'd cut myself on the barbed-wire but it didn't bleed at all. But I could see the bone at the elbow. We hurried back to the farmhouse. The older folks were not concerned at all. They got a rag dampened with kerosene and cleaned the wound. Then they wrapped my elbow with a clean rag, tied a knot to keep it tight. We kept putting bandages over the wound until it healed. I never went to the doctor or got a tetanus shot.

We visited a lot with the Robinetts, friends of Dad's from his work. The Robinetts had two sons. Once, while visiting we got to throwing rocks at each other acting like they were bullets. A rock hit me right above the right eyebrow. I bled like a stuck hog. I ran in the house, cleaned it up and put on a Band-Aid. We all got our butts chewed out for that. I had a deep scar there for a long time.

I was showing off for the girls, especially Marion Shultz, my girlfriend. We boys were jumping off a bridge onto the sand and gravel below. I'd jumped a couple of times but then I jumped and jammed my knee into my eye socket. It hurt like hell. I got a terrific black eye from that jump. Mom asked me how I got the black eye. I told her I fell off my bike and hit the handle bar. She bought it.

The big lot across the street from where we lived had no houses on it. It was vacant the whole time we lived on West Rankin. We would go over to the lot and spend many hours playing ball. We had a Shetland pony, named Smokey. Smokey would graze there.

Once Mom told me not to leave the yard, but I didn't listen to her. I went over to the lot to the end where there were a few trees and small drainage ditch.

I was milling around when all of a sudden, a bunch of yellow jacket bees swarmed and nailed me. I ran all the way home. "God is punishing you for disobeying me", Mom said. She cleaned up the stings. I think I had 23 stings all over my body: legs, arms, hands and face. The stings got red and swelled up. I looked like hell for several days.

I was playing on a swing set across the street at the Steucks house when I fell off and landed on my head. That poked a big hole in my forehead. I ran home, bleeding like a stuck hog. Mom put a damp rag on it, called Dad at work. Dad came home as soon as he could get there. He took me to the doctor and I had several stitches put in. I really got in trouble for that.

I delivered papers on my bike. Once a dog bit me in several places. They called the dogcatcher to catch the dog put it in quarantine for a period of time. Another time a dog tore my best school pants. Mom was really mad over that.

Mom got real angry with me for something, I can't remember what. She was raising hell. She had one of those paddles with a rubber ball on it that she used to spank me. She spanked me a couple of times and it broke. My mistake: I started to laugh and that really got her angry. But I think it was the last time she ever spanked me.

I earned money cutting grass for neighbors. I would cut a yard for 25 cents. There were no power lawn mowers then, just the old type push mowers. Mrs. McGrath, wanted me to do some trimming but I didn't know a flower from a weed. I got into places she didn't want me to trim. I just didn't understand, but boy did I trim. I trimmed all her flowers and let the weeds go. So much for my green thumb. I didn't get paid for that job. She told Mom about it. Mom talked to me about it, but nothing else was done.

We used to go to Fritch's grocery, it was kind of like a Quik Trip then. The small store had stuff needed for neighborhood people. People could walk in, get what they wanted and be on their way. Tommy O'Hare and I would go to Fritch's and buy a pack of cigarettes, like Viceroy or Lucky Strikes. Lucky Strikes were a very harsh cigarette and we didn't really like them. But we would sneak underneath the bridge by the store and smoke them. We also tried to smoke the lady cigars that grew on trees around there but they wouldn't stay lit. We gave up on lady cigars.

We made tree houses. One time we made a pretty substantial shed. It was partially underground and we smoked in there. We even had a little heater there to keep us warm. But we weren't very smart, the air circulation wasn't very good. The fumes made us get out from time to time so the smoke could get out.

I served Catholic Mass early morning mass at 6:00 am. I walked to church served mass for over a year without missing one morning.

I also served for funerals. One morning I was sick. I passed out and the big heavy cross I was holding fell on me. They carried me out of church. I had the stomach flu all day. I really felt embarrassed about passing out in church.

When we served funerals we would usually get a tip from the deceased family. Alter boys really thought this to be neat.

I also sang in the church boys' choir. I sang during the Christmas mass and at Christmas programs.

Before serving mass, we would have to get vials ready. One vial for wine. One for water. Sometimes we would sample the wine. We thought the wine was really good stuff. When I say we, most of the times I served mass, I served with Tommy O'Hare. We were good buddies during that time.

Tommy's dad owned a foundry. One time his dad took us both to see where he worked. A fellow there showed us how the molds were made and how the molten metal was cast. Pretty neat! But it was very hot and the smell was pretty bad. The employees working there made good money.

I played soccer with a Catholic Church team. I went to different Catholic churches and playing against other teams. The thing I remember most about playing soccer is running my ass off the entire game. I ran until I couldn't get my breath. I had fun doing it though.

My family had a pretty good size lot and a big garage. Dad was a farm boy. You know what the saying is: you can take the boy off the farm but can't take the farm out of the boy.

Dad wanted a farm so we raised chickens, calves and rabbits we butchered and sold to restaurants. We stretched hides and sold them. I spent a lot of my time working after school.

We had to feed the rabbits, chickens, livestock etc. Every Saturday, we cleaned the hutches and the food and water crocks. We used a little whiskbroom to sweep the rabbit pellets out. We had to scrub the crocks good and refill them with clean water and food.

One time Dad told me to clean out the stall where we had a calf to raise. We always butchered one every year for our food. The stall was dirty with a lot of straw, poop etc. Dad had a little trailer backed up to the door.

I started to fork the crap out. The trailer tipped at the rear because I had more weight on it. Smart-ass me, I put a 2 x 4 under the back of the trailer so it wouldn't tip. I forked the crap for most of the morning. The pile got higher and higher. I kept a close eye on the springs, they were not sagging so I thought I could just keep throwing it on.

I got the stall all cleaned out, put new straw in and was really proud of myself. Then I went over to Tommy's house. The phone rang, it was Dad. He was mad as hell and told me to get home right away. When I got home he lit into me, cussing about the springs being overloaded.

& Life Goes On...

I pointed to the springs. They weren't bowed badly at all. Dad went to back of the trailer and kicked the 2 x 4 away. I thought it was never going to quit falling. We unloaded a lot of it and had to make two loads out of it. Dad was so pissed he hit me in the back of the head with a shovel. I fell down right into the cow shit. I got the message.

One of my siblings told Dad I scratched him/her. Dad called me into the living room, he sitting on the couch. Dad pulled down my outer pants, not under pants, sat me on his lap. He used fingers to scratch both my legs deep enough to draw blood. Mom yelled at him to quit.

Dad used to generate a lot of junk by doing things like repairing or modifying the rabbit hutches, working on the chicken pens or in the big double garage. We would haul junk off to a huge, very deep rock quarry. It was the size of a city block, but when one is small a lot of things look large. I think the depth was close to 100 feet deep. We would back the trailer up to the very edge and push the junk off into the huge pit.

During that time I didn't think much about it, but if a person pushing the junk out of the trailer made one slip, down into the pit you could go. Thinking of that later on in life scared me. It would have been so easy to fall into that deep pit.

There was an empty "lot" next door, east of us. There was never a house on the property. It was owned by two brothers, I never knew their first names but the last name was Wohrman. They were German. The entire property was planted in a vineyard and was extremely well kept. We never knew where they lived, but most weekends they would be there cleaning, and mowing between rows and doing other work.

We never became close but they would talk to us and invite us over once in a while. They politely asked us to stay away from the grapes so we wouldn't damage them. We did.

However, there were four out buildings used for storage and whatever. They had no visible locks on them, but they were secured. We were fascinated by the prospect of learning how they were secured. We looked them all over, underneath, along the bottoms, under the ledges of what looked like, some type of lid. We never did find out how they were secured and locked. I don't remember seeing anyone else ever on the property trying to get into the out buildings. But we had a neat time trying to solve the mystery.

The house on West Rankin we lived in was very old, but not ancient. It had a basement under only a portion of it. One summer my cousin, Alfred Rivas and I dug out the part that Dad wanted to make a basement. We got started by crawling under the house and digging. Then we used a wheelbarrow to haul the dirt from under the house to the back yard.

Eventually, we raised the level of the back yard about six inches. It didn't look bad because we graded it by hand before we seeded it.

Once in a while Al and I would get into a dirt fight. He got so angry once, that he picked me up and stuck my head and face in a pile of dirt. I was angry at him at first but I got over it pretty quickly. Dad paid him for the work that summer and Al took a bus trip to California.

I used to go on hunting trips with Dad and his buddies. I went on a lot of coon hunting trips, staying out most of the night. I didn't get much sleep and at school I'd have a hard time staying awake. Once in a while, a nun would walk over and slap me on the head to get me to stay awake. Those nuns were mean creatures.

Dad got a baby raccoon, it was so small, that it was in a matchbox. Dad fed it with an eyedropper we called the raccoon "Scrappy"; he would wash his food in the toilet bowl.

Scrappy liked raisins, so Dad would put raisins in his shirt pocket and Scrappy would fish them out. It was really funny to watch. We kept Scrappy for a year or so, until his weight got to weight around 15 lbs.

Herman Uffman, (who was married to Verna Piocyfk) put Scrappy on his shoulder. All of a sudden Scrappy humped up on Hermans shoulder and crapped on him. What a mess. Herman came unglued, but Verna laughed so hard she had to set down.

Dad had some problem with boils appearing on the back of his neck. The doctor said Dad didn't have enough iron in his system and told him to eat raisins. Dad had a pocketful of raisins in his jumper sweater. He would reach in the pocket and eat raisins while he was working.

He stuck his hand in the pocket, grabbed a handful of raisins and put them in his mouth, beginning to chew and all of a sudden he started spitting, cussing and coughing. Dad got some rabbit pellets mixed in with the raisins. The practice of eating raisins during the hutch cleaning work ceased immediately.

I was helping clean out the chicken house one day. A mouse was running around and ran right up my pant leg. It ran around and around the top part of my pants, (below the belt). I was trying to squash it. I couldn't, so I just opened my fly and it jumped out. What a weird feeling, those little feet digging in my skin below the belt. I still feel it when I think about it even now.

I was a Cub Scout, and started with the Boy Scouts while we lived in Richmond Heights. I liked the Scouts.

The Scouts went on an overnight field trip to a state park close to St. Louis. I can't remember the name of the park but I remember the name of a cave that was there, Fishers Cave.

Fishers Cave was closed and locked over the weekend, but we found a way to climb over the gate. Several of us went into the cave as far as we could. We didn't have flashlights, so it was pretty dark and we had to go back out. We really thought that was neat. I am sure if we got caught in the cave without permission we would have been in real trouble.

The Thomas family moved to Owensville, in 1948. I graduated from the Eighth Grade, Little Flower School in Richmond Heights, Mo. I started high school at Owensville.

**Graduation: Little Flower School
1948**

I used to build model air planes. I never had much money but I was able to purchase model plane kits. These kits included: a tube of glue, a lot of Balsa strips and small panels of balsa wood.

I never had the money to purchase little engines that ran on gasoline and a little oil mixed with the gas. So I used a rubber band that came with the kit, it is what powered the plane. Also in the kit was some very thin, colored paper that was used for the wings and fuselage. There was small canister of what the industry called 'dope'. You would paint the dope on the thin paper which made the 'skin' on the wings and fuselage.

I made planes for several years when we lived on West Rankin. My mom and dad never complained about me making these models.

Eventually, I got into making larger planes. The largest one had a wing span of about four feet. The body of the plane about three feet long.

We had a big old black and tan hound that was an outside dog. One day, somebody allowed the dog inside. While he was running around the inside of the house, he destroyed my large plane. That really upset me. That was the last model plane I made.

Chapter Two:

Life in Owensville, Missouri

Moving was an experience. Dad borrowed a truck from the people he bought all the feed from for the livestock at Swift and Co. We got all the stuff in the truck. We had an easy chair to put at the top in the rear of the truck, I rode on it all the way to Owensville. That was a fun time for me.

Home in Owensville, Missouri

Living on the little farm was quite a different life style, for everyone in the family. We all had chores to do. We had to get up early every morning to milk and feed the livestock. During school months we walked to town, to school or we rode our bikes. As soon as school let out we had to get home to do chores. I was 14 years old then.

Dad got an old truck it was a flatbed Diamond T with short side boards. It was a powerhouse, a flat-head six cylinder with a five-speed transmission and a two speed rear axle. I took it to Hiram Collier's farm by the Dry Fork Creek south of Owensville to haul feed and hay for our livestock. I loaded and unloaded it by myself. I did this many times while living on the farm.

I drove the fence posts in to make our fence. Dad bought oak posts six feet tall and sharpened. We went to a logging area north of Gerald, Missouri. We loaded the posts and brought them home to make fences.

I was too short to reach the top of the posts to hit them with a 16 lb. post maul and drive them into the ground. I drug an old table around to each post I was going to drive. I stood on the table and drove the post into the ground. Dad smoked so he didn't have much stamina and could only drive in a few posts. But after he got his breath back, he would drive in another. I would drive in three or four posts to his one.

When we went to Gerald to get the posts it was July and August when we went to Gerald to get the fence posts. As we loaded them, we would sweat profusely. On the way home Dad loved to stop at a filling station in Gerald and we would get very delicious grape drinks, called Grapette. I know Dad would drink at least a half dozen of them and we boys would drink several as well.

We had a new pond dug on the farm so Dad wanted it fenced. He decided to use the steel posts for this fence. It required a different type of driver. It was a piece of pipe about two foot deep. You slid the driver up and down on the steel post to drive it in. As you drove the posts in, whether the sharpened wooded ones or the steel ones, you would hit rocks.

If you hit a rock when the post was a few inches down, or close to be all the way down, you had to pull it out and reset it. Then you started all over. Dad was a real stickler for straight lines. He wanted the posts to be in almost perfect straight lines.

When Dad came home on weekends, the first thing he would do is go check the work we had done during the week. He would eyeball the fencerows. If he found one out of alignment he would make me take it out and drive it in again. Sometimes he would get pretty mean about it.

Almost every time I would work on the fences, I would get poison ivy, sometimes pretty bad. I would get it in my eyes; they would swell up almost to the point of me not being able to see. I would sweat and the little poison ivy blisters would break and allow more poison to spread to other parts of my body. I looked awful with the red rash all over my body.

Aunt Josy, Grandma's sister, told me if I would spread fresh milk on the rash and don't wash it off through the night, it would help get rid of the rash. By golly it worked! By the next morning and the rash was already starting to scab and dry up.

The farm we bought had not been used as a farm. Consequently, the growth of sprouts and weeds had taken it over. Cutting up all the sprouts took a couple of years to finish. Dad bought some goats to help keep the weeds and sprouts growth in check.

The goats did an exceptional job keeping the weeds down. After I got all the weeds pulled and sprouts cut, we would let them dry out, then we burned them.

The goats loved to eat cigarettes. They will eat just about anything. We would really get Dad angry, when we would sneak in the house and get some cigarettes to feed to the goats. I guess if you had enough cigarettes, the goats would eat them as long as you fed them.

Dad worked in St. Louis all week. He had a sleeping room where he stayed during the week. The room was upstairs above restaurant at the corner of Vandeventer and Chouteau. It had a bed a chair and dresser, no air conditioning. It got pretty warm in the summer. I stayed with him several times. The traffic noise was just terrible, even into the night hours. I guess he got used to it. I never did. I didn't sleep well there at all.

I used to work for Joe Houska, a neighbor and distant relative of Mom's. He owned a farm adjacent to ours. I would work on the end of a crosscut saw all day and he would pay me 50 cents a day. I would clean out barns and shuck wheat for 50 cents a day.

The pay wasn't very good but during the day, we would knock off around 10am. We would go to the house where they would have a feed. There were sweet rolls with coffee or milk to drink. They were delicious.

At noon, we were fed big time. Roast beef, ham, sausage, mashed potatoes, green beans cucumbers, and gravy, homemade bread, biscuits and homemade pie. These were some of the best meals I had ever eaten. Around 3pm, we would come back inside to snack. So there were rewards to this hard work. When the sun went down, we would go home. After we did our chores at home, we would eat a great late supper at home.

Once when I was shocking wheat I felt something cold on my arms. It was a huge bull snake it scared the crap out of me. I dropped it immediately. The snake was as scared as I was. He went in one direction, I went the other.

Dad's sister Jane's son, David lived with us for a while. Jane had committed suicide by sticking her head in a gas oven. David lived with us for a while, but mom and dad took him back to an orphanage. I was not sure what happened, but all of a sudden Dave wasn't living with us any longer. Then he later was living with another sister of Dads: Emily.

Dave kept running away. He would run out to our small farm in Owensville. Dad would ask him if his mother (Emily) knew he was coming out, he would say yes. But Dad would call Emily and she wouldn't know David was there. So Dad would haul him back to St. Louis on Monday morning.

Mom had a cousin, Tony Mertle, who owned a lodge near Camdenton, Missouri called Red Bird Lodge. It was on the Lake of the Ozarks. It seemed to take forever to get to the lodge. The cabins were clean, but small, they were made of the native stone (flat sandstone). We would go visit for a week. Dad liked to fish. He had a management job and was always under stress and didn't fish much.

Tony had a fishing boat with no motor. When they went anywhere in the boat, it was rowed by oars. A one-lung engine provided the electricity at the lodge. Every evening, Tony started the engine that powered a generator. The power went to a bank of batteries. You could hear it running, like a putt, putt, and putt. It was pretty primitive, but it worked.

The hill going to the Lodge was horrific, Dad's poor old 1941 six cylinder Plymouth, could not pull itself up the hill. Tony had to hook his jeep to it and help pull it up the hill. All the passengers had to walk up the hill.

We used to go to Uncle Eldred's farm in Carrolton, Illinois. Uncle Eldred really had a neat farm. No tractor, all work was done with a team of horses. One trip to Uncle Eldred's farm we were on the road off the main highway, (called by the locals, the hard road). It was just dirt so of course when it rained the road was a solid mass of thick mud. We got stuck about a mile from Uncle Eldred's farm, Dad had to walk to the farm get Uncle Eldred. He brought the team to the road and pulled the car along to where it could again move on its own. .

We used to go to Kampsville, on the Illinois River, where they sold fresh fish, (usually catfish). Uncle Eldred just loved the fish. He used the excuse of us (the company) to go and get the fish. Then Aunt Lelia, a sister of Uncle Eldred's, would cook up a delicious meal. I still remember the wonderful tasting mashed potatoes and gravy. She was a great cook.

It was decided that I was going to ride the train from Owensville to the St. Louis Union Station. It was a neat experience. It took four or five hours to get there. The train stopped at every small town, unloaded freight, picked up mail or whatever.

Dad picked me up at the station and introduced me to Doug Carlin who was a railroad detective. Doug was huge man, having some Indian blood who carried a 38 special gun at all times while working. He told some stories of vagrants he had caught in empty boxcars. He talked of a vagrant being killed on the tracks when running to hop a freight. Doug worked the evening shift and told stories about all the events that took place around Union Station. It was really fascinating to listen to him.

I met up with a buddy, Bill Miller during this time. He was probably ten years older than me. He had an old two ton Chevy truck. It had a six cylinder engine, a five-speed transmission and a two speed rear end. Bill let me drive it when I worked for him.

I plowed many a cornfield for him to get ready to plant corn. I spent many a day out in the field from sun up to sun down, but I enjoyed it. The fresh air, the smell of newly turned soil was wonderful. And my buddy Bill to spend time with. Somehow I lost track of Bill after I returned home from the Navy.

Joe Houska loved his beer. When I worked with Joe, he never had a tractor, just a team of mules. Joe would hitch the team to a wagon and slip off to town. His wife, Mary, thought Joe was out in the field working. But Joe would be in town, drinking beer and sometimes getting very drunk.

Sometimes he would come home, forgetting that the team was in town. If someone in the bar noticed Joe was already gone, they would just untie the team. The team would come home by themselves. You would see Joe walking down the hill, swaying from side to side on the old gravel road, drunker than a skunk.

He came home late one evening and the team had already gone by and was probably already at home. We knew Joe would be coming by pretty soon. Sure enough here he came staggering down the hill with a sack on his back.

Dad was working out in the driveway doing some job. Joe hollered to Dad. Joe stopped and pretty soon he and Dad started drinking beer from the sack Joe had on his back. The beer was warm.

Other times, Joe would take the sack of beer home. Then he'd drop the beer into the well to hide it. The well,-kept the beer cool. That evening though, Joe and Dad sat alongside the road and visited. Dad wasn't much of a beer drinker and warm beer wasn't very tasty. Dad started pouring the beer out on the ground. Joe and Dad talked for a long time. Dad looked down and saw a big round puddle of foam where he was pouring the beer out. Dad stirred up the gravel under his feet to hide the foam. Joe would have had a fit if he knew Dad was wasting his beer.

Joe was killed a few years later, he was driving a tractor out on the highway and a car hit him.

We hauled water because our cistern got very low during the summer months when rain was scarce and the heat was hot. We just didn't have enough water for our use in the house and for the garden, etc. Dad acquired a horse tank. We took it to town to get water to dump into the cistern. We hauled about one load a week.

Every year Dad would have me go into the cistern to clean it. One time I was in the cistern, to clean it, and wouldn't you know it, a snake was swimming around in the cistern also. I wasn't too crazy about sharing a cistern with a snake. I don't remember what kind of snake it was, because I got the hell out of there. We finally fished it out with a line and hook.

Dad used to raise pheasants. He had a special pen with wiring on the top to keep the pheasants from flying off. I went in the pen twice a day to feed and water them. One time while I was in the pen I stepped on a board with a nail in it. The nail almost penetrated through my foot. It was a very deep wound right in the center of my right foot. I didn't want to tell Dad or Mom for fear of getting my tail chewed out. I chose not to tell anyone and kept it to myself. I washed it real good and put some salve on it every day.

Dad wanted to go squirrel hunting over at Gurley Ridge, a place where rattlesnakes were known to be in great numbers. Dad wanted me to wear my rubber boots to be better protected from the chance of being bitten by a snake. I wore the boots, but my foot was squeezed into the boot so tight that the sore on the bottom my foot was just about unbearable. I couldn't wait to get back home and get those boots off to reduce the pain. The wound got infected a couple times, it would get real red and puss came from it. But I finally got it to heal.

Eldred, Gerald and I would go skinny dipping under the little bridge on Springfield Road by our house. Springfield Road was used many years ago for hauling iron ore and smelting products between Hermann and Springfield.

So we were skinny dipping one day, and there was someone else from town there. This person whom I can't remember now, had a BB gun. I was sitting on the gravel bar by the bridge holding the gun in front of me, the muzzle pointed right at my face. Gerald reached over and just for no reason pulled on the trigger. The gun went off and the BB hit my right front big tooth. It broke it off even with the gum and the nerve was hanging down. It hurt like hell.

Mom was working in town at the time. I walked to town with that nerve exposed, I walked in the office where Mom was. The first thing she said was, "What are you doing here?" I opened my mouth and showed her the tooth. I thought she was going to have a cow. She was really angry.

She told me to go to the dentist and see what he could do with it. The dentist, Dr. Ebling, was very old and he should have been retired. He said if the root part of the tooth was not damaged he could put a pivot tooth in there. But it wasn't the case. The root was cracked and the rest of the tooth had to come out. He had to drill it out. It took four hours to get it where all the root particles were out. I had a large hole in my gum and it looked terrible. After it was over, I had to fear telling Dad about it when he got home on the weekend.

That weekend I tried to avoid Dad as much as I possibly could. I did quite well until Sunday evening when he was getting ready to go back to St. Louis for the following week's work. We were standing next to the pickup and I forgot. I smiled while he was looking towards me and he saw it.

"What the hell happened to your tooth?" Dad asked. I had to tell what happened. Of course he wasn't very happy about it all. I went through the entire summer toothless. Towards the end of August, Dad took me to St. Louis to the dentist he and Mom used.

The dentist fitted a plate, an entire plate for the one tooth. He found so much other stuff wrong with my teeth because other than going to the dentist to have the damaged root and nerve taken out, it was the first time I had been to the dentist. After fitting the plate, he pulled two other teeth because they were so bad. He said they were beyond repair. One was broken.

That plate in my mouth felt like I had a full mouth all the time. I got used to it and wore the plate until long after I got out of the Navy. The Navy did a lot of work on my teeth but they never attempted to replace the plate. Later, I had a permanent bridge installed by a civilian dentist.

I worked for a Mr. Henry Frueh, a professional carpenter. He obtained a contract in Owensville to dismantle the Old College Building made of oak and other lumber, square nails and some bricks that were used for areas like fireplace flues. If a person tried to drive a nail in any of the old wood, it just couldn't be done. The wood was so seasoned and old.

Mr. Frueh and I worked three or four weeks dismantling it. We hauled all the lumber and bricks out to his farm and stored it in neat piles. Then we covered most of it to protect it from the weather. We used crowbars and other types of dismantling tools to get it all apart. There were many huge timbers like 4 x 8's which were extremely heavy but still in great condition for their age.

Mr. Frueh was a very hard worker. Sometimes we worked sun up until sundown. I couldn't work for anybody during the weekends: Dad already had plenty of jobs he wanted done when he was home on the weekends.

Mr. Frueh was really a very nice ole fellow, I never once heard him swear and I never saw him get angry. I don't remember how much I made per hour but it was spending money.

"The Old College" Was City's First High School

I walked the perimeter fence at least once a week to check fences and look for trees or limbs that could fall on the fence and allow our livestock to get out. One day, I found a big old blue tick hound dog hanging in the fence. His rear legs and rear end were up in the air pointed upwards and his head was almost touching the ground.

He couldn't have been there too long because he was pretty spunky and not really suffering from hunger. I walked up close to him and he started growling, acting like he would bite me if I got close enough.

I wanted to try to get him untangled because I knew if I didn't help him, he surely would die. I took my belt off and wrapped it around his muzzle area so he could not bite me.

He was large and very heavy but I finally got him through the barbed wire so he could get free. After he got out, I held him by the collar while I checked him over to see if he was bleeding anywhere. I tried to calm and pet him I worked the belt off his mouth and got ready to get away should he try to bite. But he ran away from me and I never saw him again. I felt good about it though, I knew I saved its life.

We traded a calf for a 1932 Chevrolet four-door sedan from a friend of Dad's. I drove it for a couple of years. It was pretty old and the engine sounded like the pistons were swapping holes, but it got around pretty good and was reliable.

Mom wanted to learn how to drive so I attempted to teach her, but she didn't have the coordination. What an experience! I showed her several times how to give it a little gas and let out the clutch real slow. Well she would give it full throttle, and allow the clutch to release too fast. It would start spinning the rear wheels and gravel flew everywhere.

& Life Goes On...

She was frightened and confused by then. I couldn't get her to let off the gas or release the clutch. She held onto the steering wheel with the engine screaming, gravel flying, and me yelling at her to let off the gas. It seemed like an eternity but it was just a few moments. I finally reached over and turned off the key.

The car moved forward just a little, because the wheels were spinning but she was heading for a pretty deep ditch. After the engine quit Mom looked at me and said "What did you do that for"? She was angry, but I told her she was heading for a ditch and I didn't want her to drive into it.

I didn't think the old car couldn't handle this type of treatment too much so I sort of discouraged any further driving training sessions. Mom never said any more about it and I didn't say any more about driving lessons either.

Don Brown, Jim Henneke and a few others used to take the old Chevy down to Hiram Collier's farm on the Dry Fork Creek. We would spend all weekend there.

There were several very tall cottonwood trees with huge size grapevines hanging from them. We spent hours swinging on them. We never slept; we were swinging on the grapevines, fishing or eating roasting ears from Hiram Collier's cornfield. He said he didn't care he just didn't want us to waste any.

We caught fish and put them on a stringer. There was an old pole bridge crossing the creek. The pole bridge was a very temporary thing. Saplings would be cut, and laid next to each other like a bridge, autos could cross on it but it wasn't the most stable crossing. When the creek came up and flooded, the saplings washed away. Then the farmers cut more saplings and built another pole bridge. We would hang the stringer of fish between the poles. The fish would be in the water until we decided to eat them or throw them back.

When one of us would put fish on the stringer we would ask the others, "Did you take some fish off"? Because it seemed like sometimes there would be less fish on the stringer than before.

Major Thomas

After a while we all suspected that something was getting the fish. We suspected a turtle might be getting the fish.

So we dropped our fishing lines in between the poles close to where the stringer had been and sure enough we finally caught a big old snapping turtle. We pulled him out of the water and put him on top of an old fence post, so his legs couldn't touch anything to get away. We finally used him for target practice and that was the end of our fish stealer. Damn fish thief.

Sometime in the late '40s, the Conservation Department began to allow deer hunting again. For a while the deer population dwindled close to extinction in Missouri. The first season Dad and I went, I think it was 1948. The season was in December and was only open for three days.

The December season would usually be extremely cold, with temperatures well below freezing. Poor Dad would just freeze terribly. He would sit there and shake all over. Dad couldn't stand the cold. That first time I went deer hunting, the very first day, I shot a deer running along a creek about 100 yards from me. It was running broadside to me and I hit it. It fell and then got back up and started running. My heart was in my mouth from adrenaline flowing.

I ran down to the creek and started tracking it by blood drops along the way. I came up to within 100 feet of it again, it was lying down and facing me, but I didn't want to shoot into its head for fear of damaging the rack. It got back up and ran again. We tracked it the rest of the day but never found it.

Harold Thomas was a cousin of Dad's who had sons: Zane and Robert. They came to hunt with us. They lived in Carrolton, Illinois. Harold, Zane and Robert joked with each other all day long, sometimes trying to trip one another or pull other pranks on one another.

We had three great and fun days together. Harold told the story of a time when he and his sons were duck hunting at a place where they didn't have permission to hunt. The owner came on them, hollering and cussing. Zane asked his dad, Harold if the property owner was mad?

Harold said, "I guess he was mad, he waded in mud up to his ass to get us off his property. I guess he was mad."

We owned two milk cows. One was a Brindle and the other a Jersey. The Brindle was a very gentle, easy-to-manage animal. The Jersey was high spirited and a not-so-gentle animal. Mom had both of the cows named, but for the life of me today I can't remember their names.

The Jersey had a habit of swinging her head to the side and trying to butt you, especially when you were getting ready to milk or just after finishing milking. She butted me several times but it never hurt or bothered me, I sort of got out of her way.

She butted Dad several times when he milked, I would hear Dad cuss her out but that was just about all he did. Dad had a pretty short fuse and one time when she butted him, he started cussing, got pissed, grabbed a pitchfork and hit her so hard that her horn just sheared off. Blood squirted everywhere.

Dad had to get a clean sack and wet it down with water to stop the bleeding. She was a funny looking cow after that, with one horn on the right side and none on the left. But it still didn't stop her butting antics.

My brother Eldred and I were always close. I would say so still today. One day while we were milking before we went to school, I teased him about one of his girlfriends. Who it was, I don't remember. I finished milking first and walked out of the barn, stepping over the concrete threshold at the door. I was still teasing him. Then...

"Major, Major, wake up!" Eldred was saying as he slapped my face. It was the next thing I remembered. He had thrown a broom at me. The handle hit me in the back of the head and knocked me out. I think I was out for but just a few seconds before I came to.

When I fell, I dropped the milk bucket and spilled most of the milk. When I got in the house the first thing out of Mom's mouth was, "Where is the milk"? I told her I fell and spilled it. I don't think she ever knew the real reason why I spilled the milk. I guess I learned my lesson to not get Eldred too angry. Ha!

We always had hogs on the farm. We had a pretty large hog shed for the hogs to get out of the sun or bad weather. One 4th of July we had a big fireworks display by the pond. I had just one Whistler firecracker left. It would make a very loud whistle or squeal noise when lit.

As I walked back towards the house after the big display on the hill by the pond, I thought it would be neat to light the whistler and lay it on the roof of the hog house. The roof was a galvanized metal sheet with deep groves in it and ideal for what I was doing.

I would light the Whistler and it would travel towards the front of the building, squealing and whistling as it went. After I lit it, it started squealing and whistling. You never heard such a noise! All the hogs in the shed, probably 30 head, started making loud noises. They all ran out the end of the building, taking the end wall with them as they went.

The next morning, the entire end of the wall was pushed out from the bottom and boards were sticking out perpendicular. Well I don't have to tell you what I had to do that day: fix the wall. Dad was not really upset; he just said to get that damn wall fixed - now. So I did.

I liked to coon hunt a lot. Dad's coonhound, Chubby was a 'black and tan'. Dad really thought a lot of Chubby. He was a good coon and squirrel dog.

I learned how to read the dog's barks or long howls when on a coon trail. You can read barks or howls, and know whether the trail is cold or hot. Long drug out howls mean the trail is cold. Quick, constant barks means the trail is hot. I probably knew the dog's barks and howls better than Dad, because I hunted with Chubby often.

On weekend nights I went out coon hunting by myself and stayed out most of the night. Some nights I would follow the trail of a coon for miles.

Most times, I would end up on Hiram Collier's farm. We knew Hiram well. He gave Dad and me permission to hunt on the farm as long as we respected his property and livestock.

One night the trail was getting colder and colder. The times between the long howls became longer indicating the coon had eluded the dog. It was after midnight and I was getting ready to call the dog off and walk home. Just before I started to call Chubby, I heard this long terrible spine-chilling scream. It sounded like a woman screaming. When I tell the story, I still feel the hair on my neck raise. It really scared me. I had never heard anything like that in my short life.

I didn't call Chubby but in a few minutes here he came, running towards me, then running around me like he was scared or confused. I could see the hair on Chubby's back was raised. He rarely came to me on his own. Usually, I had to call him constantly to get him off any trail.

Needless to say, we both stayed on the road and headed for home. We were about seven miles from home. The next time I saw Hiram, I asked him if he ever heard a noise like a woman screaming.

"Yes, it is a black panther." Hiram said. Hiram had seen it several times running in the woods when he was working in his fields. Other farmers in the area also reported seeing the black panther in the area. I don't think I hunted at Hiram's farm again. In fact, I don't remember ever going coon hunting again.

Chubby disappeared soon after that. Dad was almost certain someone had stolen him because a lot of hunters around there knew he was a damn good coon and squirrel dog. We never saw Chubby again.

I had a blue tick hound named Racer. Sometimes, he worked with Chubby but never made as good a coonhound or squirrel hound. Racer disappeared a year or so after Chubby was gone. I found him dead on the highway. He was hit by a car. It really hurt me, we were buddies. Where I went so did Racer.

Somewhere I acquired an old 'Heinz 57' dog. He was a 'dukes mixture' so I named him Duke. He was a great little dog. He didn't get very large, but he was a great companion. We went everywhere together. He would get so mad when we would toss a rock in the water. He would dive in, get it and bring it out of the water. I don't know why or how he got on this kick. But he made every attempt to get that rock back out of the water. He wasn't good for hunting or anything else, he was just a friendly dog.

I am the one that killed him. I was backing the blue goose into the old garage, and Duke was sleeping under some of the packing that we had taken out of some boxes. I didn't know he was sleeping under the packing and I ran over old Dukie. It just made me sick.

Mom's brother Uncle Joe, and his family, came to visit us sometimes. He was one of those people who visited for a few minutes, then would holler to the kids. "Get in the car, and we're leaving".

So if we visited with our cousins, the visits were short.

One winter Uncle Joe, Aunt Francis and the cousins: Helen Jean, Pat and Rosemary, came to visit. A few minutes after they arrived, it started raining and freezing. The ice was forming quickly and the roads were getting worse very quickly.

Uncle Joe didn't pay much attention to the weather conditions. When they started to drive away they couldn't get anywhere. The roads were too slick to drive on. The ice storm continued for over a day. The ice accumulated to an inch deep on the roadways.

Uncle Joe couldn't leave so they stayed for three days. We kids had a ball the whole time they were there. We got the sleds out. Everyone went up and down our long, steep hill dozens and dozens of times. We played well into the nights.

We got a 55-gallon drum, put wood in it and had a nice warming fire the whole time we were outside. Finally Uncle Joe was ready to go. He loaded up the kids and got out. The roads started to soften up and after a lot of spinning, they got on their way. I will never forget the togetherness and fun we all had on those three wonderful days.

Chapter Three:

High School

High school was pretty much uneventful. I did the chores early in the morning and got to school. I either walked, rode my bike or after I acquired the old car, I was able to drive.

I was not the most knowledgeable student. I didn't study hard and or bring home a lot of homework. I was busy keeping the little farm running: doing chores, hauling hay, hauling water, cleaning out barns, chicken houses, driving fence posts and whatever else goes with small farms duties.

I had different part-time jobs while in high school. I worked part time for Jim Snodgrass for a couple of years. I worked after school or sometime on weekends when Dad wouldn't come home or not come home till late on Saturday.

Jim Snodgrass' Gas Station

& Life Goes On...

Jim owned the Sinclair Station. I learned to pump gas, wash customer's cars, and do lube and change oil for customer's cars. That was the start of my mechanic experience. I picked up and delivered the customer's autos for services or washing. I learned a lot about mechanics from Jim, but he wasn't the most knowledgeable.

One afternoon I was working after school for Jim, outside doing something. Wilbur Mason was washing his car alongside the building where we did all the car washing. Wilbur scrubbed the car; then I would get the hose and squirt him to tease him.

He told me to quit or he was going to do something to me. Then his threats got more aggressive. I kept squirting him and we got in to a fight. Eldred asked me if I remembered the fight years later. Then I remembered the day I beat the crap out of Wilbur Mason. I had the upper hand in the fight.

I tried to contribute to the family food supply as much as I could. At times, I took the rifle and went across the road alongside our farm, to an eighty-acre woods to hunt squirrels. I would usually come home with two squirrels. Mom would cook them and make squirrel gravy. It was a great meal.

I made a couple of rabbit traps from scrap wood and set them where I thought rabbits would be. I had fairly good luck catching them. Mom would cook them up and it was very tasty.

One day I caught an opossum in one of the traps. I put it in a rabbit hutch, not knowing what I would do with it. I put out lettuce, carrots and anything I thought it would eat, but it didn't eat. It got very skinny.

Mrs. Auferhiede, an elderly lady who was a biology/agriculture substitute teacher used her favorite words: "Of course" all the time. She pronounced it, "Of curse", every time she taught us.

She had a sister who visited from Chicago twice a year. Her sister wrote cookbooks and wanted to revise one of her cookbooks while in Owensville.

Mrs. Auferhiede asked me if I could find anyone who had a possum or a coon for her sister to try out a recipe for her cookbook. Well, need I say more? I decided I could skin out the possum and bring it to her. When I'd finished gutting it, it still had all kinds of hair stuck to it. It was about the size of a rat. It looked horrible.

I took it to my teacher's house and gave it to her. As I walked away, I felt guilty about the condition of the possum. I never heard any more about the condition of the possum.

I worked for my close friend, Bill Miller. Sometimes, I worked for his father, Herman Miller., who owned an old saw mill on the lower southeast end of Owensville, by the City Park.

I was the Off Bearer, who cut off slabs and carried very long, heavy wood. I would grab a slab, run up to the top of the slab pile, drop the slab and hurry back down the slab pile to grab another one.

The temperatures would be around 100 degrees. There was sawdust in my eyes, hair, nose and creeping down inside my shirt. It was horrible. I did this for about three months, until I finally told Herman Miller. I just couldn't hack it any more. So I quit being a Slab Bearer.

One day I found a mouse in the corner of the locker room and caught it. What to do with it?

I riffled through some teachers desks and found a roll of string. I tied the string to the end of the mouse's rear leg and went up on the balcony above the long lines of seats on both sides of the gym.

A couple of girls, including one of my best friends, Majorie Brockman, were sitting on the corner of the bench seats. I lowered the mouse to the gym floor so it could run around. The girls all jumped up and screamed and hollered. They ran off in different directions.

I didn't know what else to do with the mouse, so in study hall, I put it in one of the teacher's desk drawers. I never heard any more about that mouse.

During my high school years, I worked the hardest on the farm. I put in new fences, cleared out fencerows, cleared saplings and sprouts from the fields, etc. I have good memories of that time. I always ate good, had a place to sleep and a roof over my head. What else does a person need?

When I reached the age of 18 I went to Hermann, Missouri which is the county seat for Gasconade County to register for the draft. It was a big deal for Mom and Dad, for some unknown reason. Maybe because they had to drive me there.

Dad took off work. Dad, Mom and I went to Herman to register. Dad spent a very long time with the person who was doing the work at the Draft Board office. After a long while it was finally over and we were on the way home.

It wasn't until years later, after I learned of my adoption, that I knew why the time Dad spent with the Draft Board person was so important. Dad was making sure nothing would come out during the registration pertaining to my adoption.

Eldred, my beloved brother who was five years younger than I, wanted to learn how to play the guitar during the years the Johnny Cash song, *I Walk the Line*, was popular.

He would get about three notes close to being like the Johnny Cash song, he never did get much past those three notes. But he and I would get in the old '32 Chevrolet car whenever he wanted me to get him a bottle of Peppermint Schnapps. He just loved the stuff.

We would go back home with him sitting in the back seat strumming the guitar. I'd drink a can of beer and we'd visit all night, just enjoying each other's company.

Major: High School

I graduated in lower part of my class according to grades. The Korean War was going on then and I really didn't know what was in store for me. I was quite concerned.

Chapter Four:

Ahoy! Going to the Navy

A high school friend of mine, Donald Jett came to the house one afternoon right after graduation and suggested we join the Navy. I thought it might be a good idea because I wasn't crazy about being in the Army or Marines. I didn't want to be a ground pounder.

I thought if I had to be in the service, I might as well try to get something out of it, like learning some sort of trade. I went to the basement where Dad was candling eggs and made the announcement that I wanted to join the Navy. I still remember the look on his face. I thought he was going to pass out.

"Well bud, the navy recruiter comes to town every Tuesday. We'll go up there and talk with him this coming Tuesday". Dad said after he got over the initial shock.

The next Tuesday, we went to town to see the recruiter. Dad talked to him for hours on end. I thought they were talking over old navy stuff. I would sit in the car. For several weeks Dad, the navy recruiter and I met in town. They talked and talked. Finally I got to talk to the recruiter. He instructed me to be in St. Louis on July 15th at the Federal Building downtown at 12th and Market streets. Again after learning about my adoption, I knew what Dad was doing.

They had to come up with a birth certificate. I believe they didn't have one and that is why it took longer to actually get to the enlistment procedures done.

Donald Jett and Major Sasebo, Japan

& Life Goes On...

The morning of July 15th, Don Jett, Mom, Dad, Gerald, Eldred, my sister Marilyn and I all headed for St. Louis. I was to get my physical and orientation. If I passed my physical, I would be sworn in and shipped to San Diego, California.

We were instructed to be at Lambert Field to be flown out. We went by Aunt Francis and Uncle Joe's on the way to the airport because they lived just a few blocks from the airport.

We had a quickie lunch and off to the airport we went. In the meantime, I don't know what happened to Don. He got lost in the shuffle between the Federal Building downtown St. Louis and the airport. I never saw him again until my ship was anchored at Sasebo, Japan.

That was the first time I was ever close to an airport, let alone flown on an airplane. It was all new and very different. I was also a little apprehensive about flying but I was excited to board. Mom kissed me. Dad hugged me. So did Gerald, Eldred and Marilyn.

I boarded the plane from a walk-up ramp; they didn't have those fancy boarding ramps from the terminal. Everyone got aboard and before very long and we were rolling down the runway. The plane shook, rattled and rolled. It shuddered and was extremely noisy. I wasn't too thrilled about the flying right then, I just wanted to get to where we were going and get the flying part of this trip over.

We landed in Kansas City to take more new recruits aboard. We were there about an hour, dusk was approaching quickly. We headed for Albuquerque and landed there to fuel. The plane took off again. We hadn't been out but maybe five minutes when the plane turned around and headed back to Albuquerque. It was having some type of mechanical difficulties. We waited and waited.

When morning came, we were still in Albuquerque waiting to take off and get to San Diego. They finally sent another plane to pick us up. There was some type of generator problem. So

Major Thomas

we didn't go to San Diego we went to Los Angeles, and then took another plane to San Diego. We were about fifteen hours late. From Los Angeles we took a much smaller plane. Talk about shake rattle and roll, that little thing was horrible! Oil was running out on the wing on the starboard engine. If this is modern flying I didn't want any part of it.

After we arrived in San Diego, almost 24 hours late; it was close to 8pm. There was a bus waiting to take us to the training center. By then, it was already around 11pm, we were getting hungry so they fed us then. The mess hall smell was not good. The food they fed us looked like canned dog food, but we were all hungry. In the chow line we reached out and got a metal tray.

That is when I asked myself, what the hell are you doing here Major? After we ate, they marched us to a barracks and made us all take showers, then assigned every man a bunk. When I showered with a bunch of other guys, I realized I had lost my single and private identity.

I thought I was going to have to eat out of these metal trays, and take showers with other guys around for four years. It was unsettling.

It was at least midnight before we got to bed. At 4am somebody came in and started yelling and rattling his batten against our bunks. We all hopped out of our bunks and hit the deck. With barely any sleep we were on the go again. That day we got haircuts, almost shaved. We got a bunch of shots.

They issued each of us a sea bag, clothes which we had to stencil our names on every piece of, except the socks. We stenciled all our white hats, inside. All together there were 100 men and we made up a new company, number 585. Our new 'mother/father' who would take us all the way through boot training, was a Chief Romer.

Chief Romer was close to retirement, his rate was boilermaker. He was a pretty nice fella though. He didn't give anyone a hard time unless you constantly goofed up. We went through all the motions of training: short order drills, miles and miles of marching, rifle training, and shipboard drills on the USS Neversail, a land-locked wooden ship made especially for training purposes.

After about three weeks at the training center, we were shipped to a place in the desert called Camp Elliot. My nose peeled just about every day from being out in the sun all day. There was dust and sand everywhere. They told us if we wanted to go AWOL to go ahead because probably no one would make it. If you didn't get lost and starve to death, the rattlesnakes would get you. I don't think anyone tried.

Every night we worked between the barracks, washing all our clothes we wore that day. We hung all our clothes on the clothesline and the next evening we started all over again. Take down the dry clothes, hang the wet ones back on the line. We took our dry clothes to our bunks, rolled them in a neat roll and tied them with little short pieces of line and a fancy knot.

The knots had to be perfectly aligned and all the clothes rolled up and put neatly on the bunk for inspection. You had better not have anything dirty or any knots out of alignment or they would make you take them outside, wash and hang them up and do it all over again.

One morning we were all rolled out of our 'sacks' earlier than usual and not allowed to go to breakfast. We all suspected something was up. We ended up giving blood that morning. We were marched out to the grinder as soon as we finished giving blood and marched all morning without anything to eat. A lot of the guys passed out while standing out on the grinder, the heat and lack of nourishment got to them.

We got our dog tags around the fourth week. We were not allowed to go on liberty until eleven weeks of training was completed.

We had to learn how to use gas masks. We had to fight fires. Thomas always ended up being the 'first nozzle man'. I never understood why I always ended up with being the first nozzle man. They gave us toothbrushes and they pulled our teeth. They

Major Thomas

gave us a comb and cut off most of our hair. We all got to saying if they issued us Jock Straps we were going to get the hell out of there.

We had a lot of target practice with M1 rifles. I was considered a sharp shooter; I guess my squirrel hunting paid off. They classified me to be qualified for landing parties or boarding parties.

Boot camp was a busy time, very diversified, never boring. I learned a lot. But I don't think I would want to go through it ever again. It either made a man out of you, or broke you. I know of two people who didn't make it. They had their parents pull some strings and got discharged. I think it was an Undesirable Discharge. That discharge would have a bearing on their character for their entire life. I wouldn't ever want that.

I graduated from boot camp in late September. We came out as an apprentice, either a Seaman or a Fireman. When one finishes the boot training they are assigned to a duty station. Either ship or shore duty. All are essential and necessary assignments.

I was assigned to the USS LST 1122. I would report aboard the 1122 after ten days of leave. Leave was optional. I took a bus home, which took 48 hours of leave time and 48 hours more to travel on return. So I didn't have very many days at home. The time went extremely fast. I spent some time with Mary Ann, my then girlfriend.

I returned to San Diego and went aboard the 1122. The 1122 was getting ready to go on maneuvers in preparation for duty in Korea. She had just gotten out of dry dock, so she was going to complete some sea trials to make sure the repairs were done correctly.

Fate had something to do with my assignment to the LST, because when I was in High School, during study hall I would get an Encyclopedia and go through it looking at pictures. I would stop when the pictures of the LST's would appear. I looked at those pictures for long periods of time and I wondered about the LST's. It is a strange phenomenon because that is where I ended up after Boot Training and I remained aboard the same LST for my entire four-year hitch in the Navy.

The USS LST 1122
Major was stationed aboard her: 3 years, 9 months
Picture Taken: San Diego Harbor 1952

Chapter Five:

The LSTs

Let me explain the importance of the LST in my Navy career. The LST was a very vital ship that helped to end World War II. In the beginning of World War II, all the British were determined to beat the Germans and end the siege the Germans had on the British Empire. Winston Churchill worked with his military Admiralty in the effort to design and build some type of ship or vehicle that could 'beach and unload military hardware and armed forces'.

They could not come up with any sort of plausible plan. So Winston Churchill sent a dispatch to President Roosevelt, to seek some assistance in designing this type of ship. A dispatch arrived in Britain November 4, 1941 with a preliminary concept plans for such a craft.

Mr. John Niedermair, of the Bureau of Ships had been involved with United States shipbuilding for a long period of time. He was very knowledgeable of the needs and requirements of any type of amphibious ship. His design was first drawn on the back of an envelope. That was the beginning of the modern day LST: Landing Ship Tank.

It would be 328 feet long, 50 feet wide, and draw a full 13 feet draft when fully loaded. The first LST slid down the ways, one year after the very first sketch design. One thousand and fifty LSTs were made for the war effort. They were first essential crafts that beached the beaches at Normandy. LSTs were used for the duration of the war with many successful military landings. Without them, the war effort could have lasted many more years with added deaths.

Building an LST

The number of LST's required for the war effort was over one thousand ships. The Cornfield shipyards on the Illinois and Ohio rivers sprung up to build them. The Dravo shipyard built over 700 LST's. Over 200 were built in Evansville, Indiana.

When the LST's were launched from the Cornfield shipyard into the Ohio River, they were sailed up river, given the preliminary sea trails. If everything functioned as designed, they would tie a broom on the mast indicating a 'clean sweep' meaning the sea trails were satisfactory. These ships were accepted by the US Navy right there on the spot.

Major Thomas

The LST's were so well designed with many contingency or back up mechanisms installed. There were a large number of void spaces and void tanks. All this combined to make the ships almost unsinkable.

The planning of contingency events included events that might take like the ship being left high and dry and unable to get off the beach due at low tide. Another contingency event might be: how would the engine run without sea water or if the water was, as in many cases, yards behind the ship.

They designed the LST to use water to cool engines from special ballast tanks alongside the engine rooms to recirculate the sea water in these tanks to cool the engines until the ship was back out to sea. There was a mechanism in the steering room for manual steering should the hydraulic steering components fail. They had manual mechanisms set up should the hydraulic bow door controls failed.

The many void tanks along with the shallow drafts, made it almost impossible to sink unless a direct bomb, torpedo, or mine hit would damage it enough to take on a lot of water. There were diesel fuel tanks between the outer ballast or void tanks. Any WWII enemy, would not want to waste very expensive torpedoes on a LST. We had what was called 'Degausser' which repelled magnetic mines. During World War II and the Korean War these mines a menacing threat to all ships.

The illustration on the next page depicts the basic prototype design of the first LST's built in 1942. There have been many design changes and modifications since this prototype.

The picture demonstrates the research needed to make the LST such a versatile, effective war machine.

& Life Goes On...

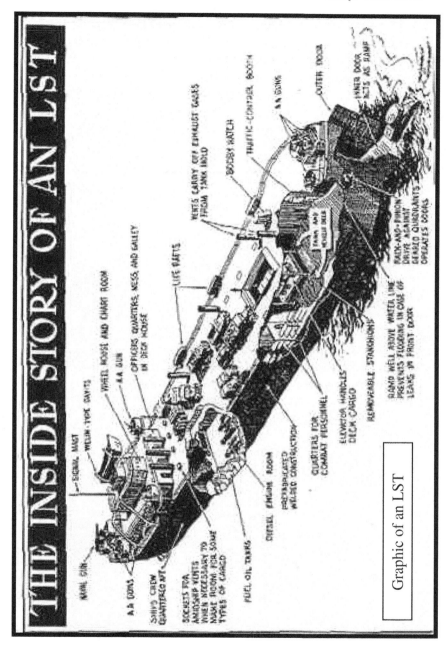

Graphic of an LST

Major Thomas

The LST's primary duty was to haul tanks and equipment. If an LST hauled thirteen Sherman Tanks, their engines had to be running while the ship was approaching the beaches. The exhaust fumes were so deadly that all the personnel in the tanks and on the Tank Deck would not have survived. Therefore an effective ventilation system had to be developed. The pictures below show the mockup of an LST and how the ventilation system was developed.

This is the equivalent of having the bow doors open.

The long view of the LST building clearly reveals the current shape.

& Life Goes On...

The landlocked LST mockup was built at Fort Knox, Kentucky in 1942. The ventilation system was developed then. Huge vent fans in large diameter tubes, were installed for when the tank engines were running. All three of the LST's generators had to run because of the large amounts of electricity required to run the ventilation system.

The detailed engineering work of John Niedermair, the contracted architectural firms and the Dravo Pittsburgh inland shipyard built the first LST with the approved ventilation system designed at Fort Knox.

The building used for the research was later used for classrooms to training military personnel. The buildings are still at Fort Knox. They are now a part of the Patton Museum of Calvary and Armor and honor The U.S. Armed Forces and World War II General George S. Patton.

I served aboard the LST 1122 for 3 years and 9 months. After about two weeks on board I was approached by a chief engineman and asked if I would like to transfer to the Engineering department and become an engineman. I asked him why he picked me. He said they reviewed my aptitude tests and they showed I was mechanically inclined and would probably be a good candidate for training in the engineering department. I said yes because I thought there wouldn't be much I could learn that would help me in civilian life by remaining in the deck department.

After I agreed to the transfer, I was taken forward to the engineering department quarters.

I taught myself about all the mechanical apparatus aboard ship. I went down to the main engine room, the propulsion of the ship. I learned about: the piping, valves, pumps, generators, batteries, fuel transfer, lube transfer and cleaning purifiers. No one in main engine room spent any time with me or answered my questions. I had three years to learn it all.

Main Engine Room

I spent many hours in the engine rooms learning as much as I could about the auxiliary and main engines. I really enjoyed this work and was somewhat trained by fellow engineering shipmates. Engine rooms not only had engines in these spaces but literally hundreds of valves, pumps, purifiers, switches etc. I was very fascinated by the way these components were interconnected to make the ship function. I learned how to make repairs, complete preventative maintenance. I would spend many hours 'on watch' when the ship was underway or when at anchor or tied alongside a pier.

In the auxiliary engine room (the generators and pump room), there were probably 50 different types of valves for diesel fuel, ballast, lube transfer, purifier operation. Three superior six-cylinder engines generated all the electricity required aboard ship. Two engines ran most of the time.

The temperature in the engine room was above 100 degrees. The only times the temps fell lower was in the winter when it was minus 35 degrees outside. The engines would suck that cold air four decks down the escape trunk.

I learned about the valves and pipes, that were used to trim the ship, called ballast. I learned to transfer diesel fuel from the main diesel fuel storage tank to the 'day tank', the fuel had to be purified to remove water, rust of other impurities to safeguard the engine's injectors.

After a year or two aboard ship, shipmates were automatically transferred. New shipmates were assigned to the 1122 and had to be trained. But I was never transferred I stayed aboard ship, full-time at my assigned duty station: the U.S.S LST 1122. The chief engineer or engineering officer never gave me instructions about any engineering components for any part of the ship. I guess they figured I would stay aboard forever.

**Engine Room 1
The Front of the Engines
Pictured here is Harold Overton,
A Lifelong Friend**

LVT's

We transported a lot of amphibious tanks, called LVT, Landing Vehicle Tank. They were considered tanks, but not with the very thick armor like Sherman tanks. LVT's floated.

They debarked from the ship on the water. There were hatches and valves to close before launching, because they went below the water surface, then bounced up like a cork.

We were launching LVT's for a beaching exercise in Hokkaido, Japan. One LVT dropped in the water and didn't surface. Luckily, the five-crew members escaped with their lives. Someone was probably in a lot of trouble for this. Later, I heard a salvage tug went to the scene and retrieved it.

The LVT's had an aircraft-type liquid cooled engine. It was extremely noisy. During the operation, one of our peter boats broke down on the beach and I had to go to the beach to fix it. I rode in an LVT to the beach, crouching behind the rest of the crew right in front of the loud engine. It was deafening, I couldn't hear for the next week. I thought the trip would never end. But I got the peter boat repaired. The throttle linkage had broken so I operated the engine by hand.

loading tanks aboard the ship

Chapter Six:

Navy Life

General Quarters was a condition set when war training began or when actual war conditions existed. I was assigned to a 20mm anti-aircraft gun. I was a First Loader. My job was to put a heavy magazine up to the gun - even while it was firing. The noise, along with the percussion, was very loud.

Later, I was assigned to a 40mm twin mount anti-aircraft gun. The rounds were much larger with only four rounds in each clip. A clip weighed 40 lbs. You lift those up to put in the guns and after a while, you get extremely tired. The noise and percussion on these mounts was almost numbing. After spending a long time on these mounts you couldn't hear very well, sometimes for days. (The VA now confirms that is the reason I am suffering with unending ringing in the ears.)

I was put in charge of the Auxiliary Engine room six months after I was transferred to the Engineering Department. The diesel engines in this engine room produced the electricity for the entire ship. Three engines could run at one time or if the demand was less, one engine might be required.

The Auxiliary Engine room was also the pump room. All the fresh water, diesel fuel, lube oil and salt water, for ballast control and engine cooling, were controlled from there. I think there were over 50 valves in this room that controlled all the pumps. There were valves for small pipes; and valves for piping as large one foot in diameter. These pumps could transfer 1000 gallons of water in one minute. I would stand watches in this engine room on a daily basis.

Major Crane Operator

Later, I was assigned to the main engine room during General Quarter's conditions as throttle man. There were two diesel engines in this engine room, with 900-horse power output. Then I was put in charge of the Auxiliary Engine room. So I worked and spent my time in both engine rooms.

Then I was put in charge of the topside machinery, which included the two peter boats, (LCVP), the topside crane, the smoke generators, and any other equipment they felt like would come under that assignment.

If that wasn't enough, I was assigned as shipboard 'Oil King'. This duty consisted of me keeping the ship level, by controlling the ballast distribution. I controlled and maintained constant inventory of all liquids, engine lubricating oil, fuel and fresh water.

I presented to the captain every morning the inventory figures of all liquids. He monitored the fresh water supply very closely. He would make his decisions accordingly as to whether we would begin to make fresh water from seawater using equipment called evaporators.

These evaporators took in seawater, heated it to a boiling point and then took the steam and condensed it. Fresh water would be the end result of this process. The evaporators running required all three generators to be on line to carry the excessive load the evaporators needed. Should any fluid inventory figures I presented to the captain be questionable I would find out why and report back to him. I can't remember any time the figures were out of line.

Anytime the Captain would notice the ship not on an even keel he would locate me and say, "Thomas she is bubble off. Get her leveled up".

Up on the bridge was a thing called an Inclinometer, which showed the level of the ship. I had one in the engine room to use as a guide when pumping ballast to level the ship. I would pump water from a side ballast tank or pump water into a side ballast tank to maintain this balance. If the captain could not locate me, he would call over the PA system, "Thomas, she is a half bubble off."

I knew right away to take care of this. It couldn't wait. The captain expected it to be done immediately.

My duties aboard ship covered just about everything. Here's a list of my duties to give you some idea of how I spent my hours aboard ship.

Duty No. 1

The 'log room' was a special room on the lower part of the ship with shelving to store mechanical machinery records for the entire ship. All mechanical repairs, however small, were recorded on the individual machine's log record. I took the time to teach new people how to maintain the records properly.

I made out repair orders to be turned in to the 'yard' people for any repairs or testing that needed to be done. So I was the person who maintained these logs.

After I was aboard around three years, they assigned a new person to me to free me up for other duties. But as time went by (around three years aboard), people automatically assumed I was responsible for all machinery.

Duty No. 2

The 'Oil King' is responsible for all liquids aboard ship. Every day I 'sounded' the fuel storage tanks and gave the captain readings. This revealed how much fuel was used in a single day. The fresh potable water reports went to the captain daily about how much water was consumed aboard ship each day.

I was responsible for the trim of the ship meaning, which ballast tanks were full of sea water and which ones were empty. The captain would have me fill or pump out any tank he wished.

Ballast tanks important if the ship 'beached'. First the tanks might be partially emptied to allow the ship to go further up on the beach. Then we might pump out more water to lighten the ship and let it slip off the beach. Pumping ballast tanks were filled and emptied by two 1000 gallon per minute Gardner Denver pumps. All three generators had to be online to supply the amount of electricity required by these pumps.

Duty No. 3

Though I didn't have formally assigned duties by the chief engineman or engineering officer, it was taken for granted that I was fully responsible for the auxiliary engine room. The generator and pump room.

Duty No. 4

I was also responsible for the main engine room, the propulsion engines. This entailed maintaining the huge engines and all attached mechanical components.

Duty No. 5

I was fully responsible for the machinery topside. This included the two LCVP peter boats that were powered by a single six cylinder diesel engine. Also the smoke generator, the high volume pumps and the old junky crane, that was powered by an old-time continental gasoline engine.

No one else was assigned to me for me to train until I was discharged.

Our engineering officer dropped the ball while in Sasebo, Japan. The Captain asked him if there was enough lube oil aboard. He said yes, there was. But when we arrived in port in Korea, we were extremely low on lube oil.

The engineering officer was about to get court martialed, he had to find more oil somewhere. An AKA supply ship was anchored in the harbor, so the engineering officer got two pallets of five-gallon cans of oil.

The temperature was around zero on Christmas Eve day. My job was to pour the lube oil into the one-inch pipe leading three decks down to the lube oil tank. The oil was thick because of the bitter cold. For three days, all I did was pour that oil into the small pipe. And Heaven forbid if you spilled any!

A third class engineman, who assisted me in the auxiliary engine room. He smoked a big thick heavy porcelain pipe like one you might imagine an Englishman smoking. When he finished his shift, he'd load his pipe with tobacco and put it in a drawer so it was ready for work the next morning.

Sometimes we would take his pipe out and drip a couple of drops of diesel fuel in the tobacco. The next morning, we'd watch him light the pipe and a puff of black smoke would come out. He would just made a funny face and kept on smoking. Looking back, I realize it was a mean thing to do.

Another time, an engineman was trying to adjust the overhead on one of the generator engines. The engine was running at 1100 rpm when he took the rocker covers off. The engine was doing what it was supposed to do while running at high speed, it was bathing the upper valve train with oil. He tried to get his screwdriver into the slot of the adjuster. There was oil dripping off his cap and his shirt. He was drenched in oil. He just couldn't get his screwdriver into the adjuster at that speed. I wanted to tell him to take the engine off line and run it at idle speed to make the adjustments. But, I didn't want to get too close because I'd get bathed in oil.

The skipper came into a port where two ships tied to one buoy. He came in too fast and close. We bumped against the moored LST. He bent the stanchion on the port side under the midships 20MM gun tub. Nothing was said about the accident.

As soon as we went to sea he summoned my shipmate Madrid and I. He ordered us to repair the stanchion and throw the bent one over the side. Madrid and I worked most of the day repairing it. We had to put a 4" x 4" angle iron under the gun tub to support the gun tub, cut off the bent stanchion, make a new stanchion and weld it to the gun tub and deck. We then painted it and looked like new. The Captain never entered the accident in the ship's log, just like he didn't log the fire I almost died in.

We had this old junky crane aboard to assist in getting heavy supplies on board. It was on the main deck, secured by heavy chains and clamped in what were called 'elephant feet'. Depressions were cut in the deck in neat rows across, fore and aft to secure equipment while underway.

The engine in the crane was a six cylinder, flat head continental. If it sat for a good while, the valves would rust and corrode, then it wouldn't run. I would remove the head and all the valves. They wouldn't come out easily because the stems had started to rust. I'd pry them out, cleaned, reseat and reinstall them. Then I reset the valve clearances, clean the block and head, and install a new head gasket. Then it ran fine until the next time. If it had sat a long while, then the same thing would have to take place again. What a tired old machine.

We took on pontoons, which required pumping salt water and transferring water from side to side. Sometimes we even had to move fuel from one side of the ship to the other to get the required list to take on the pontoons. The pontoons weighed 100 tons each. Getting the first pontoon on was not too hard. After hanging 100 tons on one side, it was difficult to move enough fuel and water to counter balance the 100-ton weight and get the required list to take on another. Some days I spent all day getting this accomplished.

When in a friendly port, I served as the engine man, which was part of the boat crew on the LCVPs (peter boats). These transported personnel from the ship to shore to conduct ship business or for movie runs or liberty calls. Many nights, I would be up all night as crewmember making numerous trips from ship to shore. The ship would set up a schedule for all ship mates. For instance, if it took a half hour to get from the ship to shore, so a set up could be for a turnaround for one trip every hour. That didn't relieve the boat crew because we were on duty for that 24-hour period. So I was on a double duty status not only to keep the peter boats running, but to make sure all the other duties I was responsible for were maintained.

Chapter Seven:

The Trip to Korea

I will never forget arriving in Pearl Harbor. It is a sight. We had survived a terrible storm, so land was a welcome sight. We arrived at Pearl Harbor sometime in the early afternoon. There was a rain shower right before we arrived so the clouds were moving out. The ocean water was a beautiful clear, deep blue. The green of the island contrasted the straight rows of yellow and orange pineapple plants resting in the rich brown soil. With the background of clearing blue sky, it was a sight I will never forget.

We were only allowed Cinderella liberty while at Pearl Harbor because Japan was still occupied by United States and other occupational forces. The Japanese were still resisting at some locations so security was extremely tight.

Some Japanese people at Pearl Harbor still harbored a grudge and were considered a risk to be around. Some of these Japanese people still harbored hatred towards the U.S. military. The military insisted all personnel going ashore pair up.

We went ashore to have fun and usually got 'plastered'. The problem was when we came back to the ship we were still pretty drunk and looking for more fun. One night after we got back to the ship with nothing to do, somebody suggested we sneak in the captain's quarters and piss on the deck by his bunk. Today, I don't see what fun that could have been, but we snuck in the captain's quarters and started to do something. Then we heard a noise. Low and behold, the skipper was in his bunk. That scared the hell out of us! We ran like the devil to get out of his cabin. We thought for sure he probably saw who it was and we were in real trouble, come morning. We went below decks and hid. But nothing ever happened. He either didn't see us or didn't say anything.

Another night wound up tight and came back to the ship. There was nothing to do so we decided to slide down the garbage shut. We would slide off the chute, land in the water, swim over to the pier, climb up the ladder there, come aboard the ship and do it all over again. We were all yelling and raising hell. I am surprised the Officer of the Deck didn't catch on to what we were doing and stop us. The next morning we realized how terribly filthy our white uniforms were. We had to throw them over the side. But we had fun.

Our time in dry dock was soon over, but we were tied to a pier for several more days before we left for Korea.

**Dry Dock
Japan**

It took us around 20 days to get from Hawaii to Japan. The captain passed the word over the PA system that land was in sight. We all ran up topside to see. Sure enough, you could see Mount Fuji from a distance. It was midday and the sun shining on the snow on the mountain. It was a beautiful sight.

This being the first time for many of us had been overseas. We took advantage of the time we had off and enjoyed a very different culture. We still had to travel in pairs, because of the great resentment towards military people.

We were sent to Sasebo, Japan for dry dock where we had thick wide bands installed around the seams of the ship. They were welded to every seam from side to side and around the bottom as well. I guess they thought that reinforcement was necessary since we had so many splits at the seams during the rough storm we endured during our voyage to Pearl Harbor.

We took advantage of the ship being in dry dock. We disassembled the main engines because we would be in dry dock for at least two weeks. I was put in charge of this operation. The engineering officer told me a crew of Japanese people would come on board to disassemble the engines, clean inside, install all new parts inside and completely reassemble the engines.

I became involved with the Japanese boss or 'Honcho'. Several days passed but nothing was happening in the engine room. I was becoming concerned because to me, two weeks really was not a lot of time for the complete disassembly and reassembly of the two huge engines.

I finally asked the 'Honcho' about it. He said not to be concerned, it would be taken care of. The engines would be repaired and ready to run when we left dry dock. The very next day about 20 Japanese people came aboard and went to work. You never heard so much noise, jabbering, noisy commotion, there were the sounds of tools dropping and other work noises. By that afternoon the engines were completely torn down. They crawled into the engines and wiped them down. A person could have eaten off the inside of those engines. The next couple of days went by and nothing happened. Two or three days later, here they came with their arms loaded with parts and tools.

Again I heard the same types of noise. There was great commotion, but by later that evening, they had the engines

completely together. There was new oil in them and they were ready to run. We could not 'light them off' because there was no water to cool them. We had to wait until we were in the bay for test running.

If we anchored in Japanese ports like Sasebo, Yokuska for any length of time, a small Garbage Scow, would come alongside the stern of the ship. These were little scows with a very small 'hold' that hauled garbage.

They had a little one lung (one cylinder) engine. When it fired, a small ring of exhaust came out, going putt, putt, putt. They were clean and painted nicely. The wheelhouse was trimmed in white paint and everything about them was well-kept. Usually a husband and wife manned them. When they threw their lines to tie off, the guys would pull the scow further to the rear of the garbage chute.

Garbage was dumped, landing on the wheelhouse and not the hold. They would shout and raise their fists. The guys thought that was funny. I felt sorry for them but I couldn't do anything about it.

I spent many, many hours in the main engine room. When I was aboard the ship about one year, I was assigned to the Auxiliary engine room and Petty Officer in Charge. I worked many hours in the Auxiliary room, getting it in better condition and appearance. Later on assigned as throttle man, and stood most of my watches in the Main engine room

The Japanese yard workers could weld. They used welding rods about three feet long and about the size of a pencil. They would stand, strike an ark and run the bead until the rod was used up. They dropped to their knees when the rod got closer to the end without ever breaking the ark. They could lay a beautiful bead.

They welded upside down and perpendicular. They worked all day for very little money. When they came aboard in the morning, they carried a bright, shiny little pails about the size of a gallon can. When finished the day's work they would go to the fantail, (very rear of the ship), where the garbage was, they would scoop their little buckets into the garbage and take it home to eat.

'Honcho' and I struck a deal. I gave him a pack of cigarettes and he brought me a bottle of Akadama wine every morning. This went on for the full two weeks, so I had a pretty good supply of wine. I hid the wine in behind the machinery manuals in the log room. I felt pretty safe about hiding the wine there because no one ever looked there. I was the only one who had any business there. I had about one half case of wine before we left the dry dock.

After all the welding was done and the other dry dock work was completed, they filled the dry dock with water. Then they opened the gates, and we were ready to float on out. The 'Hancho' and his crew were there when we lit off the main engines to check for any problems. The engines ran great. They ran for over a year without any problems.

We loaded ammunition, topped off the fuel and fresh water tanks. We loaded 100, fifty-five gallon drums of aviation gasoline, along with rice and other supplies in preparation for the trip to Korea.

loading the main deck
The main deck is loaded with barrels of aviation fuel. Below decks were tanks, jeeps and other vehicles.

We immediately started hitting the beach islands surrounding the peninsula of Korea to supply the guerillas on these islands.

This map on the next page of North and South Korea identifies the places we beached and visited during the tour of duty in Korea.

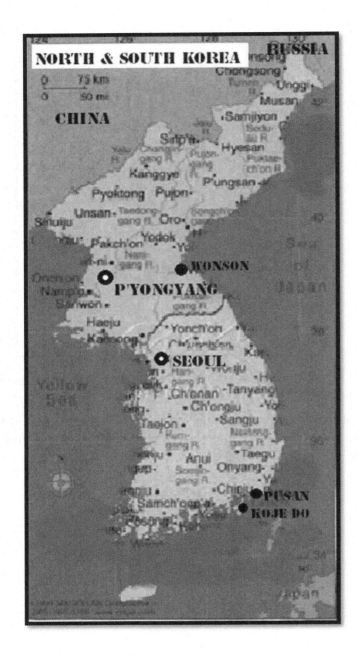

Chapter Eight:
War Zone: Korea

We arrived at Inchon, Korea. I learned that Korea and only one other place in the world, has the highest tide. We entered an inner harbor for the night. It was a very large area with locks for us to enter. It was like a harbor in a harbor. When the tide went out, there was no water for several hundred yards. We looked like we were land locked.

The real world of being in a war zone meant a completely different life style. We kept all hatches closed during night hours to keep the enemy from locating us. We got up every night at midnight for 'Bed Check Charlie'. 'Bed Check Charlie' was a patrol and spy plane that took pictures and checked on what was going on. We shot at it every night. So when General Quarters was sounded, we manned our guns and went through the motions of shooting at it. We finally learned to just stay up until 'Bed Check Charlie' made his rounds, then go to bed.

We were quite uneasy because over 100, fifty-five gallon drums of high-octane aviation gasoline on the main deck. What a wonderful target that would have been for 'Bed Check Charlie'.

The next morning, we struck out for small islands unknown to make landings and unload supplies. We usually arrived at the islands at night. We had to lower: a peter boat, LCVP, landing craft, vehicle and personnel. The boat crew consisted of the Coxswain, Bowman and the engineer. I was the engineer, along with a ship's officer. We had to make contact with someone on the island, to make sure the island was not occupied by enemy troops. That could be embarrassing to the skipper, if we beached and unloaded supplies for the enemy.

After making contact, we went back to the ship, reported to the skipper and informed him it was okay to beach. We would stay in the peter boat and lay off until the ship was ready to back off the beach so we could help in case the ship was stuck.

When the ship hit the beach they would drop the stern anchor about 100 yards out and hope it would be in a position to help us pull off. Sometimes when the tides were not just right, we could not get off. We were either too late for the highest tide or just didn't get a good hold with stern anchor for the ship assistance to dragging us off. When the stern anchor was used to pull the ship off, the huge motor required all three generators to be on line. When the motor on the winch was being used, you noticed the lights dimming as the engines worked to keep up with the demand.

If the stern anchor did not pull the ship off the beach and the anchor would drag. They would winch it all the way in then the peter boat would try to pull or 'kedge' the stern anchor as far as possible from the ship. Then drop the anchor and hope it would catch well on the bottom to pull the ship off the beach. The anchor itself weighed about a ton and half, but the real weight was the one and half inch diameter steel cable attached to the anchor. The cable resistance came from a huge drum that would not let the boat pull the anchor as far as was needed for an effective drag.

As many times as we beached and unload supplies, we had to kedge the stern anchor many times. We would make attempt after attempt and sometimes never getting the ship off the beach. The only option we would have then was to sweat it out, hoping the enemy or Bed Check Charlie didn't see us and drop bombs on us. We sat there like sitting ducks, with aviation gasoline or ammunition aboard.

& Life Goes On...

Peter Boat aka LCVP

Sailors use much slang, and worse. But the name 'Peter Boat' is a slang name that was given to the LCVP's, the Landing Craft Vehicle Personnel. The LCVP was designed and built by Andrew Higgins. Over 23,000 boats were built, mainly for WWII. They were built in New Orleans. These boats were made of plywood and had a General Motors six-cylinder diesel engine for propulsion.

Once while at one island, we made a beaching and didn't get off in time. We were stuck on the beach and had to wait about twelve hours for the next tide to come in to try to get off. We were very concerned about our situation because of the cargo on board. We had completed the preliminary work of contact with the people on the beach and were running late on getting the cargo off-loaded and getting off the beach with the tide. It didn't work out so we were stuck.

We kept all outside lights off and couldn't go out. After dark we went off battle stations but still remained on high alert for the rest of the evening. We tried to get back to a normal routine, but we had to show the nightly movie in the mess hall instead of outside on the main deck. I was watching the movie when I noticed the house lights blinking indicating there might be something wrong with the generators.

I ran to the Auxiliary engine room. All three generators were spewing steam from the expansion tanks at the front of the engines clear back to the switchboard. The engines were Hot, Hot, Hot! I ran to each generator engine and flipped the throttles to the stop position, killing all three of them. All the lights went out through the entire ship. The person who was on watch had been frantic, trying to keep the engines from overheating by turning valves and anything else he could think of. I just hoped he hadn't already completely smoked the engines.

He had opened the wrong valves, which was pumping the coolant water (sea water from the ballast tanks) over the side instead of allowing it to recirculate through the engines. When all the water was pumped overboard, the engines couldn't cool and they started getting hot.

During that crisis, I understood why it was so important to do a weekly check of what is called the Forward Ballast Control engine. We had to go to this small room forward of the ship, under the bow doors, check the batteries, start the Hercules engine and make sure it was in good running order. This forward engine was our lifesaver for getting out of this crisis. This engine was connected to a high-capacity ballast pump.

In the meantime chief came running down to the Auxiliary engine room and asked, "Thomas, what can we do to get these engines running?"

"I thought you were the Engineering Chief, why wouldn't you know what to do?" I asked.

& Life Goes On...

I got this picture of the life-saving Hercules Engine while visiting a maritime museum in Sturgeon Bay, Wisconsin in 2002. I didn't think I would ever see this little engine again after leaving the ship and I hadn't seen one like it for over 50 years.

He said the captain was really getting upset with the situation and we needed to do something to get things going again. I really got smart with him, I said if I didn't know I was sure he would know what to do. A long silence followed and I never got any answer from him. He finally admitted he had no idea what to do but thought I would know.

The only lights we had after all the generators stopped were small battery operated battle lanterns. I was glad we kept good batteries in them for situations like the one that had just occurred. It was really spooky walking the full length of the ship and climbing down into that small engine room with only the light of the battle lanterns.

I told the Engineering Chief I was going up to the forward ballast control room to see if I could get some ballast pumped back to the ballast cooling tank. I ran to the small engine compartment, hoping the Hercules engine would light off. I knew what valves to open to get some coolant waters from a huge center ballast tank below the tank deck to pump some of the water and get the auxiliary engines running again. If the kid on watch didn't cook the engines.

The life-saving Hercules engine lit off and was I glad. I transferred water from the huge center ballast tank, pumped plenty of seawater to the side cooling tanks, went to the Auxiliary engine room and crossed my fingers. I checked the oil in each engine, topped off the fresh water expansion tanks and hoped they would run. They lit off ok, sounded ok, I got them back on line and we had power again.

After getting all three engines running, I stayed in the engine room for a while and kept a close check on each engine for good oil pressure to make sure the engines didn't show any signs of internal damage. The crisis was over for now. But I wondered if the captain would have anything to say about this failure. I never heard anything from anyone about it.

I told the kid on watch to wash down each engine, generator, and all other components that had the dirty brown water on them. I said use a good soap and water solution to do the cleaning. I wanted them spotless when I came back to the engine room the next morning. He did a great job of cleaning and the engine room was clean, like I had always kept it.

I know the Engineering Chief was worried, because he should have gone down to the Auxiliary engine room when he knew the ship was high and dry to make sure the coolant function was working correctly. He didn't.

If the captain had ever said something to me about that, I would have told him to check with the Chief and see if he'd done his job. After that crisis, we settled back down and we saw the rest of the movie (which we probably had seen a half dozen times before). We all still stayed up, waiting for Bed Check Charlie, but I guess Bed Check Charlie didn't know we were there, because he didn't come calling that night.

We loaded army personnel I think at Numaze, Japan during the month of June. I have a difficult time remembering the exact date, the exact reason or the exact destination. I do however have a heavy heart with the memories of this particular "operation".

We loaded the Army personnel, and steamed somewhere to Korea. We were on the east side of the peninsula close to Wonson, Korea. The pictures I took have a caption written at the bottom, Wonson Korea. This was not the first time we have transported Army or Marine personnel for attacks. I have memories of many times having them on board. If we picked them up at Sasebo, Japan, we would have them aboard for a least a couple of days, during which time we would become 'friends'.

They had living compartments between the stern and our living quarters. When we walked through the compartments we would talk: we would ask them where they were from and they would ask us where we were from and so we got to know them.

Major Thomas

**Wonson, Korea
Unload for Attack**

We took this one company to the east side of the peninsula for a counter attack around the Wonson area. They had a little dog for their mascot. Many of us petted him during this travel time.

When we hit the beach, we dropped them off. Not long after we had dropped them off, 'Moscow Molly' announced over the radio the following comment.

"Well I see the USS LST 1122 just made a counter attack at Wonson. We just wanted you sailor boys to know that the entire company including the dog has been killed."

I will never forget the guys I met and talked to or the dog we petted. Those terrible words from Moscow Molly still remain in my mind. It could have been a propaganda statement and really not the truth.

& Life Goes On...

We had a peter boat lowered to go hit the beach, and make contact with friendly forces on an island. I was waiting for the officer to come aboard. We waited for a while when the officer that was going to man our boat waved for us to come alongside, so we did.

He instructed us, stating the ship had to go pick up a downed pilot immediately. The water was extremely cold so time was of the essence. There was also the threat that harm could come to him if enemy forces saw him in the water. The ship was in such a hurry they didn't have time to take us back aboard.

It was about 9am in the morning and it was extremely cold, especially to be waiting in a peter boat. Our instructions were to stay and wait until the ship returned for us. Then we would continue with our assignment to hit the beach. We waited, waited, and waited, getting colder by the minute.

Noontime came and went, evening came and went, night fell and we were colder and colder as time passed. We kept looking toward the horizon, but no LST. The only way we had of keeping warm was to take the engine cover off of one side of the engine huddle alongside the idling diesel engine.

The engine was just idling so it didn't have the normal heat buildup, but the temperature of the engine was around 100 degrees. We walked around the bow of the boat to keep our feet and legs warm. Our feet were getting frightening cold, the three of us were afraid of frost bite.

The next morning just after daybreak, we finally saw a ship on the horizon, and we prayed it was ours. We were so glad to see the ship coming towards us. We were frozen, starving and thirsty. We had been in that boat for just about 24 hours without food, drink or warmth.

As soon as we met up with the ship, they dropped us a thermos of hot coffee, which we consumed immediately. It seemed like it took forever to get the boat up in the davits before we could get down below to warm up. We each got a shot of brandy, I

Major Thomas

guess to get our blood to circulating again. The ship hit the beach, but a different boat crew was assigned for this beaching. It took a long time for us to warm up. This was when I messed up my feet. To this day, the only way I can tell if my feet are cold, hot or wet, is to feel them with my hands.

I have such a vivid memory of that day. That night was probably one of the most terrible nights I have ever lived through. Because of my injuries, the residual of the frost bite, the VA classified me as non-employable, which means 100 percent disabled.

WONSON, KOREA

& Life Goes On...

Chapter Nine
Operation Big Switch & War Stories

You may have heard of the Operation Big Switch during the time of the Korean War. This was the result of negotiations at Pam mum Jan. It was an agreement to swap out our prisoners for theirs.

The enemy prisoners were all detained on the Island of Koje-Do which was about two days from Pusan, Korea. The plan was to build cages on our tank deck to retain the prisoners during the travel from Koje-Do to Pusan, Korea. There were ten cages built on the tank deck to hold 100 prisoners each.

Pusan, Korea, Unloading prisoners

We loaded the sick and wounded prisoners first. The Army had lines of their personnel from the prisoner pens to the beach and our ship. I didn't understand they had machine guns on both sides of the path from the pens to the ship. I didn't think that they thought the prisoners; especially the sick ones, would run. They were all on an island, a very small island. So where could they go? I guess they thought they had the security they needed.

We transported the sick and wounded first and took them to Pusan, Korea. We were one of the first LSTs to take a load of prisoners there. There were camera crews from news stations in the USA and some other countries on the beach taking pictures of the unloading.

We transferred the first load of about 1000 prisoners, mostly sick and wounded. But someone in the higher ups forgot to figure out where these people were going to go to pee and poop. They started pooping in the elephant's feet cut outs in the deck where heavy chain hooks go for securing tanks and trucks, etc. In two days travel time, those elephant's feet filled up pretty quickly. Then they started going in the corners of their pens. After two days it smelled so bad on the tank deck we couldn't hardly stand it all over the ship. The smell was everywhere. After getting the first prisoners off the ship, we used heavy pressured fire hoses to wash the entire tank deck area.

& Life Goes On...

Koje Do Korea, load Prisoners

The next trip, we loaded the ones that were not injured or sick. They were mean as hell. By then, they had built into each pen a sort of outdoor type potty framework with a honey bucket under each hole. The rub came when they had to dump them each day.

The prisoners had to use a long pipe and the bail of the honey bucket to carry it topside and dump it out. Guess when they dumped them? At Noontime, just as most of us were eating. The smell carried throughout the entire ship, even in the engine rooms. The engines sucked air down the access trunks into the engine rooms, and the smell came with it. What a terrible stink!

Loading the mean prisoners was a traumatic time. Army personnel had their long lines with machine guns from the pens to the ship, but we saw some of the prisoners break away from the line. They were shot on the spot. The Army soldiers said three broke away. The prisoners knew when they were sent home, their generals or whoever would know they had surrendered. Some of them would be shot by firing squad.

Major Thomas

The mean ones constantly tried to escape, even while aboard ship. They would start chanting, yelling and banging their chow trays against the sides of the ship and pen. They constantly made noise and screamed. The soldiers took fire hoses and turned high-pressure water on them, flipping them head over heels and totally saturating them. Then they would have to gas them. Everyone aboard ship, especially in the engine rooms had to wear gas masks because the gas would eventually creep all over. The gassing would make the prisoners sick. They would quiet down, then start throwing up. They would be quiet for the rest of the trip, because they were so sick.

After we got the mean ones unloaded, we hosed down the entire tank deck area to get the putrid smell gone. I don't remember just how many trips we made hauling prisoners but it was a hell of a job.

The last few loads of prisoners we transported were Anti Communists who knew they would be shot by firing squads when they were back in their own country. We let them have full run of the ship. They loved the movies we showed every evening. They kept asking the movie projector operator to show the movie again and again.

Koje Do, Korea, 1953

During the day, we gave them chipping hammers to chip paint on the main deck. When you turn loose a couple hundred prisoners banging on the main deck with the chipping hammers the noise becomes unbearable. We went below decks and get away from all the noise. We felt sorry for those prisoners because they knew and we knew they would probably be killed soon.

Koje Do, Korea

While out to sea, sometimes ole Thomas (me), would come up about half plastered. Nobody could figure out how this could happen when there was supposedly no hooch aboard or a place to buy it. Then the captain decided to launch a search for the hooch.

My Engineering officer knew I had it hid in the Log Room behind my machinery manuals. The Engineering officer went to the log room and took the Academe Wine up to his stateroom and hid it in one of his file drawers. Captain went to the log room and searched for it but found nothing. The search sort of died on the vine.

A couple hours later the Engineering officer came up to me, told me what went on. "Not to worry," he said, "I took it up to my stateroom. When you want a little snort come and see me and I'll give you a little." I sometimes worked 24 hours straight to keep the tired old girl on the move, so he didn't have a problem with me getting a snort once in a while. The medic aboard the ship, (not a doctor), told me I had better quit drinking that stuff or you're going to go blind, I asked him if I could drink it until I needed glasses?

The boiler quit one night around 23:00 (11pm). Of course the Chief hardly crawled out of his bunk, so I had to check it out. I figured it was going to be a long night. The boiler was fired, but the belt-driven diesel pump had quit working. I had to locate a pump in either the main, or auxiliary engine room, storage compartments.

I found the faulty pump, removed it and installed a new pump. While I was working on it, several times the galley cooks came down and ask me when the steam for the boiler would be back on line. I told them it shouldn't be much longer. I had sheet metal to reinstall and to find a new belt to install.

While I was installing the new belt the OOD (Officer of the Deck), an Ensign who was new aboard, started asking me when the boiler would be back on line. While trying to get the belt on the pump I got my thumb nail under the belt and it pulled the nail clear off. It started bleeding like a stuck pig. I grabbed my handkerchief and wrapped it around my thumb. I was under pressure to get the boiler going, the temperature was around 100 degrees and this little Ensign was bugging me. I yelled at him to get his ass out of the damn boiler room and leave me alone. I got the boiler going, went up to our quarters, took a shower and hit the sack. I figured the Ensign would write me up for insubordination, but I never heard a word about it. It took about a month for the poor old thumbnail to start to grow back.

We all spent a lot time with the boilers because of frequent failures. We monitored it closely in an effort to keep failures to a minimum. One day while at work, I found a wooden cask. The real purpose of the cask was to be used on small boats for emergency water supply. I don't know how long it had been in the boiler room, it looked pretty rugged and dirty. It was the only one I had ever saw anywhere on the ship or in peter boats. A cook and I were talking about the cask. We decided that the wooden cask would make a neat vessel to manufacture good ole 'Raisin Jack'.

'Raisin Jack' was a concoction of a lot of sugar, raisins, water and yeast. The cook said he would furnish the ingredients if I had a place to keep a close watch on it. I figured it would be safe in the boiler room where I found it since it had been there for a long time without being noticed. The boiler room was ideal because the heat there was almost unbearable around -100 degrees or above. If we sat the cask on top of the boiler it would be even warmer.

The cook and I checked it together from time to time. We tasted it with our fingers just to see if it was fermenting, but not turning sour. We let it ferment for several weeks then lo and behold here came good ole' July 4th! Was it a good reason to celebrate or what? We went to the boiler room, I told the engineering section Watch Supervisor I would stand watch that night. There didn't need to be anyone else there until morning.

We went to the boiler room sometime that evening and started celebrating. That Raisin Jack tasted wonderful. It was so good, we just kept drinking it until it was all gone. It really knocked us on our butts.

Around midnight we started to climb up a four decks high ladder. The ladder and trunk started to spin around and around. We couldn't make it up the ladder for the terrible spinning all around us. We had to sit down there and wait until we got sober enough to climb up the ladder. We spent the entire night there. Both of us got sicker than dogs, I guess too much sweet for the body. But we had a good time drinking it. We really didn't remember much about that night. And the little wooden cask, it just disappeared.

We never quit receiving immunization shots. About every six months we got some sort of booster shot or other immunization shots.

Dogs were levers that turned and wedged into the outer perimeter of the hatch. There were six dogs on each door. With all pulled tight and with the door against the knife-edge of the rubber seal, the door was extremely tight. The dogs had levers on both sides of the door.

We had a black seaman aboard who was a very muscular, well-built individual. When he got the word shots would be given that day, he would run towards the after steering room and 'dog the hatch'. So when he was in the after steering room, he'd put his feet on the bottom dog lever, hold his hands against two of the levers and put a shoulder against the other one.

It took at least four guys to work and swivel the levers open and get to him. When we would finally get into the steering room, he would usually just pass out. The corpsman giving the shots stood by while other crewmembers got the hatch open. Then he administered the shots as required. We hated to see the day when shots were administered, because it was such a hassle with this guy.

We were at anchor in Pusan, Korea after unloading another load of prisoners. The transporting of prisoners had become like a

& Life Goes On...

milk run. We made numerous trips transporting prisoners before we would anchor in the Pusan Harbor to wait for the rest of the LST's to unload. Then we would start all over again.

We were still checked every night at midnight by Bed Check Charlie so we waited up until after he showed up, then hit the sack. On this night, we had just gotten to bed, when a General Quarters alarm sounded. We all manned our battle stations, mine being the Main Engine room. I was throttle man. I thought we were being checked out again by Bed Check Charlie, but they had us light off the main engines. We were answering bells as quickly as we could. The bell changes are the Bridge calls to change the engine speeds, and forward or reverse.

The enunciators rang a loud bell every time the enunciator was rung from the bridge. Then we made whatever change the arrow on the indicator would show. The forward speeds were on the right side of the indicator and astern on the left side. The indicator was round and about 2 feet in diameter with quadrants marking off up and down on either side. The quadrants would show: stop, 1/3, 1/2, full and flank for speeds on the forward side. Everything on forward was on the astern side except stop and flank.

I had no idea what could have been going on with all the bell changes. Then Bridge told us that we were dragging anchor and we were in a bad storm, with high winds and strong currents. We were getting closer and closer to the beach and afraid where we could do some damage to the hull if we ran aground.

I answered 300 bell changes from 1am until around 6am in the morning. I made one change so fast that I killed the port engine by switching from forward speed to full speed astern. This brought the port engine to idle. I went from forward to let the air out of the forward clutch and went to astern to fill the astern clutch with air. I brought the port engine to full speed without the air clutch fully engaged, causing the over speed trip to kill the engine as a safety feature.

When this happens, you have to pull a lever to engage the starter drive and restart the engine. This only took about 30 seconds.

It happened so quickly no one really knew the port engine had died so it wasn't responding to the bell change.

Another person in the engine room records bell changes to protect the bridge and engine room should any question arise. He recorded the changes as they were carried out, but there was no mention of this engine failure.

The over-speed feature was built in to protect engines from over speeding when the screws came out of the water in rough seas. The over speed trip threw when the engine RPM reached 1000 RPM. During rough seas, a person would be assigned to each engine. They reset the over speed trip every time it would throw out, then restart the engines. This could be an ongoing duty in heavy seas.

Even with all the maneuvering going on, we went on the beach. The stern had swung around and run aground. When the storm subsided, we got underway, heading back out to where we were anchored before. We dropped anchor and secured battle stations.

The Engineering officer approached me not long after we were secured from battle stations. He asked me about the very rear, lower void tank: did it have any ballast in it or was it just left empty as a void tank should? I told him we never used it because it was a rear, center tank. Filling it with ballast would not help keep the ship at an even keel. The piping was available to pump from it or fill it through the auxiliary room, should that need ever arise.

The Engineering officer said since we had run aground, that tank may have suffered some damage. He wanted me to take him back to the after-steering room, where the access tank cover was. We took the necessary tools to remove the cover and inspect for damage. I got my big, long heavy-duty ratchet wrench and the proper size socket and a battle lantern. We took the 22 nuts off to pry off the tank cover. The oblong cover was about two feet by two feet just large enough for a person to enter. We really had to pry the cover off because it was sealed with a thick rubber gasket that had been in place for many years. It came off after a lot of prying and pulling.

With the cover off, we heard water gurgling somewhere inside. The Engineering officer said "Thomas I want you to go down in the tank and see just how bad the damage is. Let me know so I can tell the skipper."

Yea, good ole Thomas. I felt like saying if you want to know how bad the damage is, why don't you go down there and check it out. But I didn't. I got through the opening. As soon as I got further down, I smelled rust and stinky water. There was the sound of water gurgling and it was darker than the inside of a cow. It got real scary. As I write this now, I still get goose bumps on the back of my neck.

Well the damage was minimal. There was a hole in the hull right by a cross support beam. The hole was torn, about the size of a baseball. Water was bubbling in through the tear, but not very fast. The water either be pumped out or allowed to fill in even up with the water line outside the ship, and would cause no problems.

I climbed back out, put the gasket and cover back on with the 22 nuts and retightened it all. The Engineering officer reported to the skipper. They decided to let water fill up to even with the outside water level and get it repaired in dry dock. Around 11am, I went up topside. I hadn't had any sleep and after the scary job of checking the tank, I was ready for a smoke and get my wits together.

When I talked to the others aboard, we discussed the storm and all the work we did to keep us from getting into worse trouble than we did. They said to look out to the huge rock formations on the perimeter of the harbor and note the two tall mast looking objects. That was what was left of the new freighter, the Cornhusker.

Major Thomas

Cornhusker, on the rocks, Pusan Korea

The Cornhusker had run aground and broken in half on those jutted rocks. What a mess, oil slick and 'beer' floating on the water. She had been on her maiden voyage. She sat there on the rocks for a long while. We'd see her when we entered port.

But one day we entered the port and the Cornhusker was gone. The Japanese ship builders had come. They covered the open areas with a thick canvas, filled her with air and floated her. They towed her to Sasebo, Japan.

The Japanese put her in dry dock. There was still blood in some of the state rooms when we went aboard her while she was in dry dock. So there had been injuries.

The pictures of the Cornhusker, shown on the next page were while she was in dry dock. There was: the bow section, in dry dock, and the propeller. Matched to the size of scale.

These give a good idea of what size she was.

The Japanese ship builders put her back together. I heard the cost was over 1 million dollars just to re-tube the boilers. She was an impressive sight.

We returned to our homeport, San Diego, California after serving our first hitch in Korea. Most of the crew was offered a fifteen to eighteen day leave. No one was allowed any thirty day leaves because the Korean War was still in progress. Of course I chose the eighteen day leave. I decided to take a train home instead of the uncomfortable bus. On the train, you could walk around and take a meal any time. I took the train to Hermann, Missouri.

Chapter Ten:

Liberty

Once on liberty several of us were hanging out and needed to know what time it was. We stopped a Japanese person and asked him the time. He looked at us with a deadpan look.

"I am sorry but I don't speak English." He said, in perfect English.

Sometimes between trips to Korea some of us were allowed three days of R&R. We made plans to take a train somewhere into mountainous area about three hours from Sasebo. We arrived at our destination in the afternoon and were taken to a very upscale hotel and spa. All six of us were all assigned to one large room with six small beds.

We walked around the small town for a while before dinner at 6 PM. The dinner was served in a large room like a restaurant. We sat at a long table with a large group of Japanese people. We sat on one side of the table facing Japanese men across from us. They nodded and smiled.

The food was served, but we were told by our officers not to eat any greens because the Japanese used human fertilizer. I don't remember what else was there to eat, but we finished the meal.

The Japanese men tried to converse with us but we had a very difficult time communicating. The waitresses brought in a small porcelain vase. We weren't sure what it was or what they contained. Then, the waitress brought small porcelain shot glasses. These glasses were much smaller than an American shot glass. The Japanese men giggled, as they poured the liquid into the shot glasses, then toasted us.

We poured our shot glasses and toasted them. It was very warm and had a very pleasant taste. Needless to say, we drank all what was in the vases and asked for more. We got more. Before long we were drunk.

Later, we found we were drinking 'Hot Sake' or rice wine.

At dark, we went to our room and ordered beer. They brought it to us. Some guys tried to get the waitresses to come into the room, but they weren't stupid. When we ordered more beer, they made us come downstairs and get it ourselves. We were pretty-well plastered.

My bed was parallel to large windows at the front of the hotel. The next morning, I woke up to giggling. The Japanese people were pointing up towards me: giggling and laughing. I realized I was lying on the outside concrete ledge: Naked! I didn't know how long I'd been out there. I was so embarrassed. I jumped back into the room, onto my bed. I couldn't live that down for quite a while.

That morning, we walked along a road leading out of town. There were a half dozen or more horses being held by their owners or handlers. They were renting them out, but the horses remained with their owners. The owners lead the horses up the mountain that had six to eight switchbacks on the trail to the top.

At the top, there was a small building with souvenirs, beer and tee shirts. We got off our horses, drank a few beers and enjoyed the view. Drinking the beer at that higher altitude got us into an inebriated state. When one of the guys mounted his horse, he stepped in the stirrup and went right over the other side of the horse, falling on his butt.

After we started down, several of us broke loose from the owners and raced the horses down the mountain. The owners ran through the switchbacks yelling and raising their fists. When we got at the bottom the owners arrived a few seconds after we did, out of breath and really angry. Really angry.

& Life Goes On...

We had a good time there and the three days went by quickly. The trip back on the train was uneventful. I think the time off done all of us a lot of good.

Seaman VanMeter, married in San Diego right before the ship departed for another tour of duty in Japan and Korea. We arrived in Yokuska, and he went on liberty by himself. He never made it back to the ship. The CID on the base in Yokuska was notified because foul play was suspected. His body was found about a month later floating in the bay with his throat slit. That is why the ship's officers mandated that no one go on liberty alone.

I went on liberty with a bunch of fellows to Tijuana, Mexico for a night on the town. We were heading for Japan and Korea once again. Well we got to drinking 'Cubra Libras', (rum and coke). We all got pretty well plastered.

Sometime during this drinking bought, I got into an argument with a cab driver. I wasn't going to pay him. The argument got more intense and it wasn't long before the police were there. They were getting ready to haul my ass off to jail. Thank God my Engineering officer came by. He told me to get my ass out of there or I would be locked up and maybe never get out. I did.

I don't know what time I got back to the ship, but I had to take on fuel and top off our tanks. I went below and supposedly lined up the correct valves. I yelled to the dock people and told them to go ahead and start pumping. Well, I had some valves wrong. As soon as they started pumping the fuel came over the side.

To cover my ass, I yelled at them and something like you guys must have connected to the wrong piping. They bought it and I got my butt out of a jam. So I went below and just opened valves to fill a different tank. I could have been deep trouble for polluting the bay.

Major Thomas

The first of December of 1952, my boss the engineering officer, asked me if I wanted to take the rest of leave I had coming. He said I had to come back before Christmas though. I thought about that for some time. It would be extremely difficult to be returning to the ship right before Christmas. But I had a thirteen-day leave.

I purchased a round trip bus ticket and went home. The time went very swiftly, I spent time with Mary Ann. The days just flew by before it was time to return to San Diego. I still remember that mournful day.

I went through the same thing every time I was getting ready to go back to the ship. There was the trip downstairs with Dad. He had something to tell me, but never did. Then there was the trip back to Cuba, Missouri to meet the bus. Not much was ever said. Now, I think they assumed Dad told me I was adopted and that I was dealing with the news.

> —FA Major F. Thomas, Jr., left Wednesday for San Diego, California, after spending ten days' leave with his parents, Mr. and Mrs. Major F. Thomas, and brothers and sister. He is stationed aboard the USS L. S. T. No. 1122, now in port at San Diego, California. The No. 1122 is due to leave shortly for the Asiatics.

That day at the bus station, I waited for the bus, the sun was sinking in the west and it was bitter cold. I got on the bus and waved back to them. They waved to me as the bus drove off the family fading away as they stood in the distance. It was a dreadful time. I really had a hard time getting through it. Everyone was getting into the Christmas season, but I was leaving to go back to duty, then on to Korea.

After I left the Navy, I found out that I was adopted. I know now Dad was going to tell me I was adopted. I don't know how I would have handled him telling me then, having to get on a bus and leave. It was hard enough.

While we were on liberty somewhere in Japan, several of us got pretty well plastered. We were at a lumberyard and jumping off stacks of lumber. Then we got a hold of a pole, like a telephone pole. The cops were running after us and we were still holding on to the pole. We ran up the gangway and dropped the pole. All of us disappeared, running below decks to hide.

We all took off our uniforms and crawled in our bunks, pretending to be asleep. The OOD and cops came through the compartments but they didn't find us.

I got over leaving home pretty quickly because we had a lot of hard work to do as soon as I was back on board. We had to top off all our fuel, fresh water, and lube oil tanks. It was a very busy time.

If my memory serves me correctly, we departed for Japan and Korea either right after Christmas or right after the first of the New Year. We were out to sea about five days when we hit a tremendous storm. We were with the LST flotilla, I think five other ships. We all sustained some damage. We obtained 121 cracks in the bottom of the ship at the seams. We could stand in the engine room and see water seeping into the cracks. It was not a real problem our bilge pumps could keep up with the water coming in. Some of the LST were damaged worse than ours. Several LSTs lost peter boats, some lost masts and other outside rigging. As soon as we arrived in Pearl Harbor we had to go into dry dock for repairs. The cracks in the seams were welded. We were in dry dock for over two weeks.

Major
Cuba, Missouri Bus
Station
December, 1952

& Life Goes On...

Chapter Eleven

Duty Keeps Calling

Many times when we were anchored in ports like Inchon or Pusan, Korea or even at some islands, we saw Rocket Launchers shooting at the mainland or to other islands. Rocket Launchers were converted LST's. It would take over 24 hours to load all the launchers and just 20 minutes to fire them off. Rocket Launchers would expend their entire supply of ammunition in about 20 minutes because the launchers fired so quickly.

After loading and until the launchers were fired, Rocket Launchers had more fire power than a Battleship, but only for 20 minutes. Unfortunately, there was no way it could maintain this firing power for long due to lack of load space and lack of time to reload. We saw and heard the battleships the USS Missouri and the USS New Jersey, fire towards the mainland or other islands.

The USS Missouri and the USS New Jersey were of the Iowa-Class battleship. They were armed with nine 16-inch guns. They were 887 feet long and had a beam (width) of 108 feet. The draft was 36 feet. They displaced 57,000 tons when fully loaded with ammunition, supplies, and full fuel.

They had four General Electric turbine engines, with eight boilers cranking 212,000-shaft horsepower. Their fuel was a heavy type of fuel oil. They were completed in respectively: in 1943 and 1944.

You could see the huge orange, yellow fireball coming from the 16 inch gun rounds overhead. Then you would hear a dull whistling sound. Several moments later you might see the explosion and then hear the explosion off in the distance. The weight of a round fired was about the weight of a Volkswagen automobile. The round could travel as far as 25 miles away. When a 'broadside' was fired, the ship would move sideways about six feet. These ships were huge and commanding.

One evening in Inchon Harbor, a tug was tied alongside of us. It was just a small sea-going tug. When Bed Check Charlie came over, all ships would fire at him. Our gunners were never that good so they could never hit him. But the little sea-going tug next to us with just 20mm guns, hit it and downed him. We tried to claim we hit it but that wasn't the case. We had to admit we didn't hit it. The next night, another Bed Check Charlie was taking his place. It never ended.

If a crisis situation occurred, I was called by ship's officers, or sometimes the captain. If a peter boat wouldn't start or run: call "Thomas". If a main engine quit running: call Thomas. If the crane wouldn't start or run: call Thomas. If the mess hall had to be painted: call Thomas. If the ship listed to port or starboard: call Thomas. If a compartment flooded: call Thomas. If diesel fuel, lube oil or fresh water had to be taken aboard: call Thomas.

I got to know another cook and we had the bright idea to make another still. He was able to come up with a shiny five gallon (tin) that had milk in it. When it was emptied, we took it to the main engine room, drilled a small hole in one corner at the top and put a ¼ copper tube all the way to the bottom of the can.

We had a glass thermometer in the tube to monitor the temperature. If it were too cool we would put more steam to it. If it was too hot we would shut off the steam. We put an old funnel on the can upside down. Then we found some rubber hose and ran the hose all the way to topside to allow the

'fermentation smell' to go topside. We hoped it wouldn't be discovered. For several weeks, we monitored it and couldn't wait to try it.

One day I thought I had better check the raisin jack for curiosity sake. I found rust in it. That ended that engineering feat, it had to be thrown overboard. The only good that came of it is the very next day the port engine developed a flywheel problem right where we had the still.

The Captain came to the engine room to check this flywheel problem out. Thank God we threw the still overboard the day before. Whew!

While over in Korea area after beaching on an island and backing off, the Captain wanted me to check a forward void tank directly behind the chain locker, below the tank deck ramp. I removed the cover (these have 20 big nuts), and inspected the tank for possible fuel leaks at an expansion joint of a fuel pipe that ran through the void tank.

There were no fuel leaks, but we found a very slight salt-water leak into the tank at a seam weld. I had to 'sound' all void tanks and report any changes of fluid levels to the captain, even if there were no significant changes.

I had the cover off, waiting for the captain to decide if any action should be taken before resealing it. All of a sudden the ship started to get underway. Immediately a foot-high wall of water started coming in over the ramp. The 'Bow Doors' weren't secured properly so the wall of water came in with such force that it ran into the hole where the cover was off. This created a tremendous vacuum at the opening. If I hadn't moved quickly I would have been sucked into that tank.

It really frightened me and I was caught off guard for a moment or two. I had to regain my composure and do something quick because if the tank deck flooded, the ship would run lower and lower in the water. It could have sunk the ship. I ran like a crazy person 200 feet to the rear of the tank deck and found a sound powered phone at the rear of the tank deck. From a half deck, I called the bridge and told them they had better stop the ship immediately, we were taking on water fast in the tank deck.

The engines came to an idle and the ship stopped but the water was still coming in. It was slower but the ship had lowered into the water quite a bit. The captain sent the chief Bo-swain's mate along with some deck hands to get the water out. They had to get a couple of 'Billie pumps' in there to pump it out.

The void tank was already full of water and I pumped it out. The chief Bo-swain's mate was responsible for the Bow Doors being properly secured so he was written up. I shudder to think what might have happened if I wasn't there when the water came rushing in.

We were tied up to a huge freighter in the Inchon harbor. Inchon Harbor is the one harbor they had to fill with water because of such a high tide. We were watching a movie on the main deck and evidently the movie was very boring or we'd seen it at least a dozen times.

So, we started talking with the guys aboard the freighter. After we talked for a while, we learned about what they had on. Guess what their cargo was? A full load of Schlitz beer. Do I need to say anymore?

Pretty soon we had sacks loaded with parts, boxes with parts, cigarettes and anything else we could swap for beer. The guys were hiding cases of beer everywhere. Beer was even hidden on the angle supports of the bow doors. After the swapping of beer settled down some of the guys got pretty plastered. Then, here came Bed Check Charlie on his nightly reconnaissance mission.

We all ran to our general quarters stations. One gunner's mate was so drunk he fell two decks down from the main deck to the tank deck. He got up, brushed himself off and hollered, "watch that last step, it's a bitch. He wasn't hurt just a little bruised. We were ordered to fire at the recon plane, but most of the gunners mates too drunk to hit anything. The Captain called over the sound-powered phone headset to the gunner's control to cease fire. But the drunken gunners kept firing toward the conning tower. It really got the captain pissed off. I think a couple of gunner's mates were written up for this. The Captain knew something was wrong.

I hid my beer in the forward bilge pump room. Only a few fellow engineers knew of this compartment and no one ever came there. I hid my beer under the deck plates and every once in a while, Don Bock and I would sneak down there and have a few beers. No one ever found it. We drank all the beer we had hid.

When we prepared to beach at the next island, they opened the bow doors. The doors wouldn't work right so the chief Boswain's mate climbed up the angle irons inside the bow doors. He found cases and cases of beer. The cases of beer actually got caught in the bow door opening mechanism. The Captain was really pissed. He and other officers searched the entire ship, all compartments. They found all kinds of beer everywhere. Beer was even stowed in life rafts, in the peter boats, under the stern winch and in vents, just about anywhere cases of beer would fit. They even found beer in the main engine room under the deck plates and in the main engine room parts compartment and in the boiler room. But they never ever found mine.

When we unloaded rice and other guerrilla supplies, they would form long lines from the tank deck where the rice was stored, to the beach. Then they would pass each sack of rice to the end of the line and stack it. One of the guerrillas unloading the rice was caught stealing a sack. You never heard so much commotion in your life. All of the other guerrillas ran along the beaches picking up stones, branches, and chunks of wood and formed a gauntlet, which the thief had to run through.

The thief was beaten, kicked and hit with rocks, limbs, and chunks of anything they could find. Towards the end of the run he was on his knees crawling. By the time he was close to the end he died. They just don't tolerate anyone stealing from others: especially food.

Sampans were either Chinese or North Koreans, laying magnetic mines. Most ships operating in the Korean waters had Degausers, which would set up a field around the ship making the magnetic part of the mine ineffective. But the scuttlebutt had it some sampans were sunk after mines were discovered aboard them.

Chapter Twelve

The War Ends?

Our ship was anchored in the harbor of Pusan, Korea the day the hostilities ceased, July 27th, 1953. There really wasn't much celebration because we didn't win the war. No one did, Legalities to this day say the war has never ended and no armistice has ever been signed.

We finally got back to Japan again after spending well over three months straight at sea. We were doing pretty much nothing but hitting many different islands furnishing supplies. We brought everything from aviation gasoline, rice, lumber and sometimes vehicles and personnel.

We hadn't been paid for three months. We ran out of cigarettes and had to start chewing tobacco to satisfy our tobacco needs. We got so hard up that we would look into butt cans. If we saw a butt maybe a half-inch long, we got a tooth pick, stuck it into the butt, did our best to light it and get a couple of puffs from it. We called that shooting snipes.

Then we finally got mail, after none for three months. It took forever to get it all read. Almost everyone on board received a large sack of mail. One fellow read a letter from home and found his father had passed away. He didn't even know it. We felt sorry for him. The Red Cross is supposed to contact anyone who may have a death or if someone in the family is very ill. Evidently the Red Cross didn't do its job.

The captain was very concerned about the Number One generator engine black-stacking. This is when black smoke is excessive even when the engine is under normal load. Or if the engine is overloaded and there's too much black smoke when using the stern winch.

Our captain, Lt. Wilson, was very concerned about the generator. He said something to our chief engineman about it several times. The chief would ask me what we could do about it. I really didn't answer him because I wasn't sure. I thought about it a lot and tried to come up with a solution to the problem. But if the chief knew what he was doing, he should of recommended checking the injection pump timing or maybe doing some other checks. But we got nothing from him.

We were coming into the port of Sasebo, Japan and the crew was to have three days for liberty for R&R. We tied up alongside a supply and repair ship and my wheels started turning. I went aboard the supply ship, located a supplier and asked him if he had parts for a superior generator engine. He said that he had most of the parts we would need to overhaul the engine.

I had never torn down an engine in my life. But something had to be done. I got parts I thought I'd need. I got six new pistons, ring sets for each piston, six wrist pins, six sets of rod bearings, three heads, rebuilt injection pump and all the necessary gaskets.

The supply person said I'd have to give him something of equal value before he could give me the parts. I invited him to our main and auxiliary engine room store rooms and let him decide what he could use. He saw a twelve-inch brass gate valve, which I thought we would never use so I let him take it. He and I had a hell of a time getting it up the escape trunk, through the hatch and over to his ship. We had to use a line rope to pull it up the escape trunk and through the hatch. We had just about all we could do to carry it aboard his ship.

I finally got all the parts down to the auxiliary engine room, and began to tear down the engine. Two other engines were running all the time so the temperature was about 100 degrees. We had many tools in each engine room so I didn't have a problem disassembling the engine.

I got the pistons out. What was needed to press the wrist pins from the pistons was a tool called a press. We didn't have a press aboard ship. I had to figure a way to get the wrist pins out. The pistons were aluminum and the wrist pins hard steel. I put two and two together: if I put the pistons in a bucket of steaming hot water, the aluminum would expand quicker than the hard steel pins. It worked! The wrist pins slid out easily.

I cleaned all the parts for reassembly. Having used the process for removing the pins I thought about putting the pins in ice and putting the pistons in steaming hot water, again they slid right in place. I just reversed the process to get the new wrist pins in the new pistons. No press required.

I installed the rings on the pistons, installed the pistons, new rod bearings, installed the three newly rebuilt heads and installed a newly rebuilt injection pump. Hopefully, I had timed it right - having done any of these things before.

Then I installed all new oil and fuel filters. We had many manuals for repairs etc. on the engine so I followed the procedures as closely as I could; I torqued all the components as per the manual specs.

I worked on it from the day we arrived at Sasebo, Japan around noon until the third day we were in port. The ship was getting under way the third morning just as I was finishing up. The Captain called down to the engine room and asked me if number one generator was on line. I told him it would be in a few minutes. I couldn't get one lower coolant hose on.

I was tired and filthy. I went up topside, got a breath of fresh air, smoked a cigarette went back below and the hose just went on with no problem. I checked the oil level, checked the coolant and crossed my fingers. I pushed the start button; it turned over a few times and fired up!

I checked everything I could think of, looked for any coolant or oil leaks: none to be found. Then I went to the switchboard and put it on line with the other two engines. The engine performed well. No more black smoke. The engine ran for over a year without ever shutting down.

Feeling like the engine was doing okay, I went to our living area, took off the filthy clothes and slung them over the side. It took me about an hour to get all the filth off in the shower. I hit the rack and slept for 18 hours straight. As I had worked through those three days. I was so dirty they wouldn't even let me eat in the mess hall; I had to eat on the fantail. I did receive a Commendation Mast and a Letter of Commendation for this effort.

"We were taking on water in some port in Japan. This is a stressful job because you have to go down three decks to the tanks and follow closely where the water is, then go back up topside to tell the people on the dock how much more to pump.

Well I was hurrying back down the access ladder three decks below when I missed a rung on the ladder and hurt my left knee badly. I couldn't stand for a while, and definitely could not climb back up.

The OOD, (Officer of the Deck) hollered, "Thomas you have water overflowing on the main deck. Turn off the valve!"

I yelled back to him I couldn't because I hurt my knee. He would have to come down and shut it off. I had to show him which valve to close. I had trouble with this knee a long time after getting off the ship. Even after getting married, it hurt me so bad that I couldn't sleep. I am still having problems today, with arthritis in my knee.

We were anchored at a port in Korea, preparing to head back to the States via the Great Northern Route. Roberts, a first class engineman was told to get me and make a final inspection of the main engines. We removed the hand hole covers to inspect every part of the engines we could.

The starboard engine was fine. When we got to the port engine, we found water seeping through cracks near all cylinders from the water jacket. Serious problems. I mean serious.

Roberts had to inform the engineering officer who in turn informed the skipper. What to do? What to do? Roberts, the skipper, engineering officer and myself went to the ship fitters shop to talk to Madrid, who was a full-blooded Indian.

The captain asked Madrid if he thought we could weld the cracks. Madrid said he'd take a look to see if it could be done. It was already late in the evening. The captain asked me to help him and to try our best to weld the cracks. The ship was scheduled to leave in the morning. First we had to drain the fresh water from the engine's water jacket.

In the meantime, Madrid and I went to the welder and started to carry the many feet of welding cables and ground cable to the main engine room. That was a job in itself. The cables were about 1 inch thick - very heavy. When the water was drained, we 'V-grooved the cracks with a small electric grinding wheel. The regular welding hood was too large for us to get our heads in the hand hole ports to work.

We used cutting, torch-type goggles with the proper lens to protect our eyes from UV rays. Madrid started welding and brought his head out. "I cannot make a proper bead," he said.

Another problem was Madrid, who went to welding school, suggested we reverse the polarity. But when we did that the beads were then okay. We welded all night. By morning we (hopefully) had all the cracks welded before the ship was to get underway.

We both had serious face burns, especially our foreheads and cheeks. We looked like raccoons for several days. Every day we were teased about it. But I told them if we didn't do what we did we wouldn't be on our way home.

While in port at Yokosuka, Japan, we frequented the Sunshine Bar. We'd just gotten there when there was a commotion at the door. We saw nothing but a bunch of people in 'civies' come crowding in. What was going on?

I was sitting on a bar stool and the next thing I knew, I was on the floor. We all started swinging, mainly to protect ourselves. I kicked a guy in the jaw and later on heard it was broken. McRae busted a chair over one of the guy's head; he had to have 44 stitches. When it was over the Japanese police arrived along with Shore Patrol.

We ended up at the shore patrol headquarters. We Navy guys sat on a bench on one side and the others were on a bench on the other side. Two of the guys were holding their jaws, so we suspected they had broken jaws. We sat there, waiting to see what was going to happen next, sort of joking around and talking. Several of us lost our white hats but that was about all. The other guys were sitting there not saying a word.

Eventually a Marine Corps officer came in and started chewing their butts out. In so many words he said, you are really a bunch of tough marines. Look at those sailors not a scratch on them and you all look like hell. The shore patrol was going to put us all in the same barracks that night. We all protested. We told the shore patrol the fight would resume if they put us in the same barracks. They did separate us.

In the morning the SP took us back to the ship and nothing else was ever said about the fight. The LST 1122 did have a reputation after that. Don't mess with LST 1122 crew.

All the time I served aboard the ship for 3 years, 9 months, I only remember being in the radio room once. There were all kinds of radio equipment and little motors, etc.

The ship's generators ran on DC (direct current) electricity. Some of the radios had to run on AC power, (alternating current).

The radiomen were having a problem with one of the motor generators that generated AC power. They needed parts for it and no parts were aboard so they had to go elsewhere to find the part that they needed.

They heard of a place by Tokyo, Japan where the parts might be available. I was told to go with the radiomen to help them get the part. We got a jeep from the motor pool and drove to the junkyard.

A large sign above the entrance to the yard had the following wording. The spelling may not be accurate so I will spell it as best that I can remember. *'TOXON INCHIBON JUNK'*. That means: a lot of very good junk.

The radio men found the part they needed so I borrowed some tools there in the yard, to get it apart.

While anchored at Kobe, we went on liberty and crashed an Air Force Officer dance. The next morning the captain was told to take his ship and get the hell out of Kobe. Needless to say the skipper wasn't a happy camper.

The captain received orders to proceed to Buckner Bay, Okinawa. We no more than arrived, when word came a typhoon was approaching. The ship's captains were given the choice to ride out the storm in port or leave port to ride out the storm. Our captain took the option of going to sea. The seas were already heavy when we left port.

The proper and safest way to ride out typhoons is to sail directly into the storm. Then you avoid having hundred-foot waves hitting the ship broadside. Being the throttle man for the main engine room meant I spent most of the stormy three days in the engine room manning the throttles.

If the propellers came out of the water when the stern went up, the main engine would over speed. The engine was designed to shut down automatically when the engine speed reached 1000 RPM. An over speed trip, would kill the engine. A lever would have to be pushed back into place, then starter drive lever pulled to restart the engine. This went on for most of the three days we were at sea during the storm.

We needed two extra people to man the engines and keep the main engines running. When the storm subsided, we had steamed ahead full speed forward, but lost 40 miles. The seas were so rough we were taking 70 degree rolls. We could not operate the galley so all we ate were sandwiches. There was no way we could sleep because we would fall out of our bunks. So we curled up between the Bulkhead (wall) and our lockers, (which were welded to the deck), to sleep.

Arriving back in the states around the first of July, 1956, we entered the ship yards and dry dock in San Francisco. On July 9th, when we entered dry dock. I emptied most of the ballast tanks to lighten the ship for numerous repairs. Then I transferred fuel from diesel fuel storage tanks so those tanks could be repaired.

During those days I ran all over the ship. From my log room, I worked with the yard workers to complete all the ordered repairs.

July the 10th, I was going to be discharged. The ship was leaving dry dock so the ballast had to be transferred. The diesel fuel tanks needed to be filled.

Where was Thomas? Gone.

The individual I trained for the log room work told me later at a ship reunion that July 10th was a day of horror for the the USS LST 1122. No one to pump ballast or transfer fuel. And there was no one to do the work that needed done for the ship to get underway.

I would have loved to have been a little mouse in the conning tower that day to watch the havoc. I was told that it took three people to fill my slot.

Chapter Thirteen

Mrs. Sullivan

After completing a tour of duty in Korea, we returned to our homeport in San Diego, California. I was allowed a fifteen day leave.

I was excited to visit my family, who lived in the small Missouri town of Owensville. I purchased a round trip train ticket and spent ten wonderful days with my family. The train trip took two days and a part of a third day both ways.

It was a hot Sunday in July when I was to leave and return to my ship. Sunday morning we went to Mass at church. My mother wanted to make homemade ice cream before I left for San Diego. But I insisted there was no time for homemade ice cream. We needed to leave immediately if so I would not miss the train.

The thirty miles from Owensville to Hermann was on a state highway in the northern foothills of the Ozarks. It was hilly, narrow, and crooked. I was afraid we would not arrive at the station in time.

Fortunately for me, the train was five minutes late. My family and I stood on the platform and said our goodbyes as the train approached the station. I hurriedly got on board, found a coach seat by a window; and waved to my family. The train pulled away from the train station.

The train moved quite slowly at first. I regained my composure after the hectic driving trip. I noticed a lady walking toward me in the aisle. She stopped at my seat, then looked at me for a few seconds. She had watched me saying my goodbyes, hugging and kissing my mother, shaking hands with my father and hugging my siblings. She had tears in her eyes because she knew it was a hard time for my family, and for me.

She knew I was either going into the service or returning to my duty station.

"Yes; I am returning to my duty station at San Diego, California." I said. I went on to explain that I served aboard a ship, the LST 1122. But she seemed to be more interested that I was a sailor rather than the specifics of my duty.

"Would you mind if I sat with you?" she asked.

I invited her to sit down. She tried real hard to help me forget the pain of leaving my family. She was so tender and compassionate. She made me think that she needed me as well.

We ate every meal together. She insisted on paying for each meal during the long train ride back to my naval base.

After several hours of small talk, our conversation became more personable and comfortable.

"Where are you bound, and where have you been?" I asked her.

"I'm returning from Norfolk, Virginia," she said. She had just christened a ship there. Then she told me about losing her five sons during World War II.

This helped me understand why she needed comforting, too.

As we rode along, she told me the story of how her sons gave their lives for our great country. The tears streamed down her cheeks. She wiped them away with a handkerchief. I reached over and put my hand on hers. I wanted so much to comfort her. I will never forget the two days we spent together on the train.

Near Los Angeles, the time came for us to go our separate ways. She gave me her address and asked if I would write her. I told her I would. Then I gave her my address.

A few days later, the crew of the USS San Joaquin County, LST 1122, departed for Korea again. I wrote several letters to this fine lady, but never heard from her. I don't think all the mail went through. Sometimes, we went for several months without

& Life Goes On...

receiving mail. I think our letters just never got to where they were supposed to go.

We were scheduled to depart for Korea and Japan and I really didn't have the time before we departed to write. I did write on the way over to Korea. I assumed the mail would go out as soon as we arrived in Japan. But we immediately departed for Korea so I'm not sure if the mail left our ship to go stateside.

I have fond memories of Mrs. Sullivan. Hardly a day goes by that I don't think of Mrs. Sullivan and her five sons. She was the mother of the five Sullivan brothers.

Two ships have been named after the Sullivans: a Fletcher class destroyer and U.S.S. The Sullivans 537. It went into service December, 1943. The second U.S.S The Sullivans, DDG 68. Guided Missile Destroyer went into service April, 1997.

The Sullivan family lived in Waterloo, Iowa.

The two oldest brothers, had each finished a tour with the U.S. Navy in May 1941. But after the bombing of the Pearl Harbor on December, 7th, 1941, all five brothers decided to join the Navy to serve their country.

They had to get special permission to allow all five to serve on the same vessel.

Their picture on the next page shows the announcement made when they were declared missing in action.

Mrs. Sullivan

& Life Goes On...

The Sullivan Brothers
Mrs. Sullivan's Sons

Major Thomas

The Story of the USS Juneau

After stopping briefly at the Tonga Islands and New Caledonia, she rendezvoused 10 September with Task Force 18 under the command of Rear Admiral Leigh Noyes, flying his flag in WASP (CV 7). The following day Task Force 17, which included HORNET (CV 8), combined with Admiral Noyes' unit to form Task Force 61 whose mission was to ferry fighters to Guadalcanal. On 15 September WASP took three torpedo hits from the Japanese submarine I-19, and, with fires raging out of control, was sunk at 2100 by LANSDOWNE (DD 486). JUNEAU and screen destroyers rescued 1,910 survivors of WASP and returned them to Espiritu Santo, New Hebrides, 16 September. The next day the fast cruiser rejoined Task Force 17. Operating with the HORNET group, she supported three actions that repulsed enemy thrusts at Guadalcanal: the Buin-Fasi-Tonolai Raid; the Battle of Santa Cruz Island; and the Naval Battle of Guadalcanal (Third Savo).

The ship's first major action was the Battle of Santa Cruz Island 26 October. On 24 October HORNET's task force had combined with the ENTERPRISE (CV 6) group to reform Task Force 61 under the command of Rear Admiral Thomas C. Kinkaid. This force positioned itself north of the Santa Cruz Islands in order to intercept enemy units that might attempt to close Guadalcanal. Meanwhile, on Guadalcanal, the Japanese achieved a temporary breakthrough along Lunga Ridge on the night of 25 October. That short-lived success evidently was a signal for enemy surface units to approach the island.

Early in the morning 26 October, U.S. carrier planes uncovered the enemy force and immediately attacked it, damaging two Japanese carriers, one battleship, and three cruisers. But while our aircraft were locating and engaging the enemy, American ships were also under fire. Shortly after 1000 some 27 enemy aircraft attacked HORNET. Though JUNEAU and other screen ships threw up an effective AA barrage which splashed about 20 of the attackers, HORNET was badly damaged and sank the next day. Just before noon JUNEAU left HORNET's escort for the beleaguered ENTERPRISE group several miles away. Adding her firepower, JUNEAU assisted in repulsing four enemy attacks on this force and splashing 18 Japanese planes.

That evening the American forces retired to the southeast. Although the battle had been costly, it, combined with the Marine victory on Guadalcanal, turned back the attempted Japanese parry in the Solomons. Furthermore, the damaging of two Japanese carriers sharply curtailed the air cover available to the enemy in the subsequent Naval Battle of Guadalcanal.

On 8 November JUNEAU departed Noumea, New Caledonia, as a unit of Task Force 67 under the command of Rear Admiral R. K. Turner to escort reinforcements to Guadalcanal. The force arrived there early morning 12 November, and JUNEAU took up her station in the protective screen around the transports and cargo vessels. Unloading proceeded unmolested until 1405 when 30 Japanese planes attacked the alerted United States group. The AA fire was devastating, and JUNEAU, alone accounted for six enemy torpedo planes shot down. The few remaining attackers were pounced on by American fighters; only one bomber escaped. Later in the day an American attack group of cruisers and destroyers cleared Guadalcanal on reports that a large enemy surface force was headed for the island. At 0148 on 13 November Rear Admiral D. J. Callaghan's relatively small Landing Support Group engaged the enemy. The Japanese force of 18 to 20 ships, including 2 battleships, far outnumbered and outgunned his force, but did not outfight it.

American gunnery scored effectively almost immediately sinking an enemy destroyer. JUNEAU teamed with ATLANTA (CL 51) to destroy another as the two forces slugged it out at close range. During the exchange JUNEAU was struck on the port side by a torpedo causing a severe list and necessitating withdrawal. Before noon 13 November, the battered American force began retirement. JUNEAU was steaming on one screw, keeping station 800 yards on the starboard quarter of the likewise severely damaged SAN FRANCISCO (CA 38). She was down 12 feet by the bow, but able to maintain 13 knots. A few minutes after 1100 three torpedoes were launched from the Japanese submarine I-26. JUNEAU successfully avoided two, but the third struck her at the same point which had been damaged during the surface action. There was a terrific explosion; JUNEAU broke in two and disappeared in 20 seconds. The gallant ship with Captain Swenson and most of her crew, including the five Sullivan brothers, was lost. Only 10 members of the crew survived the tragedy.

JUNEAU received four battle stars for World War II service.

& Life Goes On...

The Sullivan Brothers
Mrs. Sullivan's Sons

Major Thomas

The Story of the USS Juneau

After stopping briefly at the Tonga Islands and New Caledonia, she rendezvoused 10 September with Task Force 18 under the command of Rear Admiral Leigh Noyes, flying his flag in WASP (CV 7). The following day Task Force 17, which included HORNET (CV 8), combined with Admiral Noyes' unit to form Task Force 61 whose mission was to ferry fighters to Guadalcanal. On 15 September WASP took three torpedo hits from the Japanese submarine I-19, and, with fires raging out of control, was sunk at 2100 by LANSDOWNE (DD 486), JUNEAU and screen destroyers rescued 1,910 survivors of WASP and returned them to Espiritu Santo, New Hebrides, 16 September. The next day the fast cruiser rejoined Task Force 17. Operating with the HORNET group, she supported three actions that repulsed enemy thrusts at Guadalcanal: the Buin-Fasi-Tonolai Raid; the Battle of Santa Cruz Island; and the Naval Battle of Guadalcanal (Third Savo).

The ship's first major action was the Battle of Santa Cruz Island 26 October. On 24 October HORNET's task force had combined with the ENTERPRISE (CV 6) group to reform Task Force 61 under the command of Rear Admiral Thomas C. Kinkaid. This force positioned itself north of the Santa Cruz Islands in order to intercept enemy units that might attempt to close Guadalcanal. Meanwhile, on Guadalcanal, the Japanese achieved a temporary breakthrough along Lunga Ridge on the night of 25 October. That short-lived success evidently was a signal for enemy surface units to approach the island.

Early in the morning 26 October, U.S. carrier planes uncovered the enemy force and immediately attacked it, damaging two Japanese carriers, one battleship, and three cruisers. But while our aircraft were locating and engaging the enemy, American ships were also under fire. Shortly after 1000 some 27 enemy aircraft attacked HORNET. Though JUNEAU and other screen ships threw up an effective AA barrage which splashed about 20 of the attackers, HORNET was badly damaged and sank the next day. Just before noon JUNEAU left HORNET's escort for the beleaguered ENTERPRISE group several miles away. Adding her firepower, JUNEAU assisted in repulsing four enemy attacks on this force and splashing 18 Japanese planes.

That evening the American forces retired to the southeast. Although the battle had been costly, it, combined with the Marine victory on Guadalcanal, turned back the attempted Japanese parry in the Solomons. Furthermore, the damaging of two Japanese carriers sharply curtailed the air cover available to the enemy in the subsequent Naval Battle of Guadalcanal.

On 8 November JUNEAU departed Noumea, New Caledonia, as a unit of Task Force 67 under the command of Rear Admiral R. K. Turner to escort reinforcements to Guadalcanal. The force arrived there early morning 12 November, and JUNEAU took up her station in the protective screen around the transports and cargo vessels. Unloading proceeded unmolested until 1405 when 30 Japanese planes attacked the alerted United States group. The AA fire was devastating, and JUNEAU, alone accounted for six enemy torpedo planes shot down. The few remaining attackers were pounced on by American fighters; only one bomber escaped. Later in the day an American attack group of cruisers and destroyers cleared Guadalcanal on reports that a large enemy surface force was headed for the island. At 0148 on 13 November Rear Admiral D. J. Callaghan's relatively small Landing Support Group engaged the enemy. The Japanese force of 18 to 20 ships, including 2 battleships, far outnumbered and outgunned his force, but did not outfight it.

American gunnery scored effectively almost immediately sinking an enemy destroyer. JUNEAU teamed with ATLANTA (CL 51) to destroy another as the two forces slugged it out at close range. During the exchange JUNEAU was struck on the port side by a torpedo causing a severe list and necessitating withdrawal. Before noon 13 November, the battered American force began retirement. JUNEAU was steaming on one screw, keeping station 800 yards on the starboard quarter of the likewise severely damaged SAN FRANCISCO (CA 38). She was down 12 feet by the bow, but able to maintain 13 knots. A few minutes after 1100 three torpedoes were launched from the Japanese submarine I-26. JUNEAU successfully avoided two, but the third struck her at the same point which had been damaged during the surface action. There was a terrific explosion; JUNEAU broke in two and disappeared in 20 seconds. The gallant ship with Captain Swenson and most of her crew, including the five Sullivan brothers, was lost. Only 10 members of the crew survived the tragedy.

JUNEAU received four battle stars for World War II service.

USS JUNEAU

Length: 541.7 feet (165.1 meters)
Beam: 53.15 feet (16.2 meters)
Draft: 20.7 feet (6.3 meters)
Displacement: approx. 8,340 tons fully loaded
Speed: 32.5 knots
Aircraft: none
Armament: 16 12.7cm 5-inch/38 caliber guns in eight twin mounts, 12 x 28mm guns, 8 x 20mm guns, eight torpedo tubes
Crew: 63 officers and 785 enlisted

Crew List:

This section contains the names of sailors who served aboard USS JUNEAU. It is no official listing but contains the names of sailors who submitted their information.

USS JUNEAU History:

USS JUNEAU was laid down by Federal Shipbuilding Co., Kearny, N.J., 27 May 1940; launched 25 October 1941; sponsored by Mrs. Harry I. Lucas, wife of the Mayor of the city of Juneau; and commissioned 14 February 1942, Captain Lyman K. Swenson in command.

Following a hurried shakedown cruise along the Atlantic coast in the spring of 1942, JUNEAU assumed blockade patrol in early May off Martinique and Guadaloupe Islands to prevent the escape of Vichy French Naval units. She returned to New York to complete alterations and operated in the North Atlantic and Caribbean from 1 June to 12 August on patrol and escort duties. The cruiser departed for the Pacific

Chapter Fourteen

Navy Records

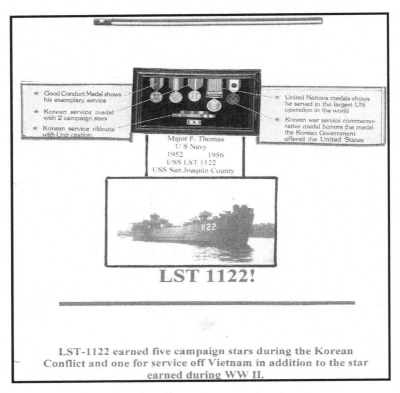

The USS LST 1122 AKA The USS San Joaquin County.
The Japanese would refer to the ship as ICHY—1 NEE --2
The verbiage being "ICHY-ICHY NEE—NEE."

> **ADMINISTRATIVE REMARKS**
>
> U.S.S. SAN JOAQUIN COUNTY (LST-1122)
>
> COMMENDORY MAST:
>
> 3 August 1955:
>
> For meritorious service performed while attached to the U.S.S. SAN JOAQUIN COUNTY (LST-1122) during the period 1 December 1954 to 1 August 1955; Engineman Third Class THOMAS distinguished himself by his strenuous efforts in doing all tasks assigned him well foregoing sleep and regular meals to follow his jobs to successful conclusions.
>
> His industry, initative and loyalty are an inspiration to the crew and contribute to the accomplishment of all jobs assigned to the ship.
>
> Specifically, while assigned as petty officer in charge of the Auxiliary Engine Room, he devoted much of his own time in painting, cleaning, and working on equipment, greatly improving the material condition of this space.
>
> As Petty Officer in Charge of the log room, he keeps the log room in an excellent condition of organization, appearance, and preservation, again using much of his free time.
>
> Engine Third Class THOMAS's cheerful and unfaltering devotion to duty is in keeping with the highest traditions of the naval service.
>
> H. R. DUTTON, LT. USN
> Commanding Officer
> U.S.S. SAN JOAQUIN COUNTY (LST-1122)

I was awarded a Commendory Mast by the Captain. I also received a letter of Commendation. I was to report with undress blues the following morning for the presentation in front of the entire crew. See commendation letter above.

Major Thomas

The following sheet was my evaluation of rate, proficiency in rate, seaman ship, mechanical ability, leadership, and conduct.

DATE	REASON	RATE	4. PROF. IN RATE	5. SEA-MAN-SHIP	6. MECHAN-ICAL ABILITY	7. LEADER-SHIP	8. CON-DUCT	SHIP OR STATION	INITIALS
25 OCT 1952	P	5	UNDER INSTRUCTION				4.0	NAVTRACEN SDIEGO	
31 DEC 52	Q	SA	3.5		3.3		4.0	USS LST 1122	
31 MAR 53	Q	FN	3.6		3.5		4.0	USS LST 1122	
30 Jun 53	Q	FN	3.6		3.5		4.0	USS LST 1122	
30 SEP 1953	Q	FN	3.6		3.6		4.0	USS LST 1122	
31 Dec 1953	Q	FN	3.6		3.6		4.0	USS LST 1122	
31 Mar 54	Q	FN	3.7		3.7		4.0	USS LST 1122	
30 June 54	Q	FN	3.8		3.8	3.6	4.0	USS LST 1122	
30 Sep 54	Q	FN	3.8		3.8		4.0	USS LST 1122	
31 Dec 54	Q	EN3	3.5		3.5	3.6	4.0	USS LST 1122	
31 Mar 55	Q	EN3	3.8		3.8	3.6	4.0	USS LST 1122	
30 Jun 55	Q	EN3	3.8		3.8	3.8	4.0	USS LST 1122	
30 Sep 55	Q	EN3	3.9		3.8	3.8	4.0	USS SAN JOAQUIN COUNTY (LST-1122)	
31 Dec 55	Q	EN2	3.9		3.8	3.8	4.0	USS SAN JOAQUIN COUNTY (LST-1122)	
31 Mar 56	Q	EN2	3.9		3.9	3.8	4.0	USS SAN JOAQUIN COUNTY (LST-1122)	
30 Jun 56	Q	EN2	3.9		3.9	3.8	4.0	USS SAN JOAQUIN COUNTY (LST-1122)	

NAME (Last) THOMAS (First) MAJOR (Middle) FRED, Jr.

LETTERS FROM SHIPMATES

The captain of our ship was Lt. Harold Outten.

I had to prove to VA there was a fire in storage room because Captain Outten didn't record the fire in the ship's log. I had to get letters from shipmates, not only to prove about the fire, but also to prove about: my hearing loss, ringing in the ears and about my feet being dead from frostbite.

I wrote over thirty letters to fellow shipmates who served at the same time I did and asked if they remembered the fire. Thankfully two fellows did, they wrote the VA and verified it.

The Events Surrounding Thomas Extinguishing the Storage Room Fire

When the ship is at port where liberty is allowed, it was common practice for one shipmate to ask another if he might 'Stand By' so he could go on liberty. The person requesting the Stand By, must not ask anyone who is unqualified. In other words, they must have the same qualifications as the requesting shipmate.

When I was asked to Stand By, I didn't have the same qualifications as my shipmate who requested this. When the fire broke out, I had to extinguish it. But I wasn't familiar with an 'OBA', an apparatus that changes exhaled breath to oxygen.

The apparatus didn't work properly, so every time I inhaled, I took in less oxygen. Toward the end of the event, I was hardly getting any oxygen.

The person I stood by for, was a damage control crew member. I was an engineman. Therefore, he got written up for asking a non-qualified person to stand by for him.

He was restricted to the ship for two weeks. The captain ordered him to teach every crew member how to operate the OBA.

What happened to me aboard Ship

A fire broke out in a storage compartment, the Lucky Bag storage area, and two decks below the main deck. I was summoned, "Thomas, lay below to the Port shaft alley on the double".

Upon arrival at the access hatch to the shaft alley, several officers, a chief and several enlisted persons, were waiting for me. I was instructed to wear an OBA (Oxygen Breathing Apparatus) mask and harness. The harness had a snap loop on the back for a small cable called a 'tending line'. It was connected and tended by another person. This was a safety precaution in case I would become injured or couldn't make it out on my own.

When I first put the OBA on, I felt that it wasn't working right. I couldn't breathe. After every exhale, the inhale was less than before. The smoke and soot was rising above the compartment into the access passage as I descended to the burning compartment. I felt the heat from the fire. I opened the access hatch to the compartment (there was only one access hatch to this compartment) and started towards the fire.

The compartment was dark. All I could see through the smoke and soot was the yellow and orange flickering fire. Suddenly I could not move any closer to the fire because the individual that was supposed to be tending my line disappeared.

He'd gone out of the compartment, closed the hatch and 'dogged it down'. I could hardly breathe. I was about to take it off and breath without it, but I got to thinking that I would be breathing in that thick, stinking, soot and fill my lungs.

The cable tending line was squeezed between the hatch and the knife-edge and I couldn't move any closer toward the fire. I had to reach out as far as I could with the CO2 nozzle to try and contain the fire. Eventually, I got the fire out. I remained in the compartment for a while to make sure the fire didn't restart.

The heat was intense. I was so hot that I didn't have one stitch of dry clothing. I sat the CO2 fire extinguisher down and used both hands to feel my way toward the hatch, following the cable. After I got to the hatch I released all six dogs to get the hatch open. I kicked open the dogs; and he had tightened those dogs very tight.

I was getting so weak. I laid down on the deck and kicked the bottom dog open. It was so tight. My breathing was labored, like I was running up a hill. My breaths got shorter and shorter with every minute. I finally got the hatch opened so I could exit. The smoke and soot was caked all over me.

The soot was all over my clothing and my hair, it was running down into my eyes and ears. I was so weak and dehydrated from heat exhaustion. When I finally made it back up to the compartment, I literally threw the OBA off and collapsed on the deck. I may have passed out momentarily.

The damage control officer and the ship medic helped me sit up. After 30 minutes or so, I was able to get up on my own power. I was so angry with the person who was supposed to tend my line that I would have probably done some personal injury to him, but two officers restrained me.

As time goes by, I get worse thinking about this fire. If I enter a room or area and something or someone blocks that doorway: I get panicky. I get sick at the stomach and at times start to tremble if I see that the doorway is blocked. I cannot be surrounded by a lot of people without getting edgy. I have to get into the open and away from people. I have canceled flights because if I can't get an aisle seat, I will not fly. I could not stand to sit in a middle or in a window seat. I do not go to movies because of the darkness.

The end result today, Post-Traumatic Stress Syndrome, I have to take medication for depression, medication for sleep and medication for nightmares.

Years later my wife Erna, suspected that I was suffering from depression, I asked her why she didn't say something to me about it and she said she didn't know how I would take it.

The VA people asked me how I could drive eighteen-wheelers with my feet suffering from the residual of frostbite that I obtained from serving in temperatures of 35 degrees below zero with just low cut shoes and dress socks. At times, I'd stayed out in those temperatures for 24 hours.

Then, the VA dermatologist found Melanoma on my back and wouldn't let me leave the hospital. I told her we were going to a reunion. I offered to come back as soon as we returned from the reunion. The day I got back, I went to the VA and they removed it.

The doctor told me if I had let that go for six months, I would've either been on chemo or dead. That really scared the hell out of me. They saved my life.

They called me, and sent a letter confirming it was melanoma. I had to go back so they could remove one more millimeter around the first incision to make sure all the melanoma was gone. Then, I got a clean bill of health: no more melanoma.

During the process of filing my claim about the fire on the ship, about the crisis with the ship running aground, my hearing problem and ringing in the ears. They had to verify all of my statements.

The VA obtained a ship's log and wouldn't you know it - the skipper did not enter the fire or the accident when he'd pulled alongside another LST and hit it. The ship's captain didn't enter anything in the log about the ship running aground.

& Life Goes On...

The VA also needed verification. So I wrote 31 shipmates and asked if any of them remembered the fire, the ship running aground, or anything about me being left in minus 35 degree temperatures when my feet were frozen I received some very helpful replies and sent them to the VA.

01-29-05

Dear Fellow Ship Mate,

My name is Major Thomas. I served aboard the USS LST 1122 from October of 1952 through mid July of 1956.

I ended up Engineman 2nd class. My duties consisted of the following. Log room yeoman, oil king, in charge of the Auxiliary Engine room and in charge of topside machinery.

I have been working with the VA for several years in an effort to receive disability for Post Traumatic Stress. (PTSD). The VA has tried to validate my story of the fire aboard ship through the National Archives and ships records. Nothing in the ships records show evidence of a fire in the Lucky Bag compartment. I am going to send a copy of my Stressor Letter, describing the actual event in detail. I know how the fire started, ship fitters and the ships welder Ishmeal Madrid, were doing some torch cutting and welding in the compartment forward of the Lucky Bag. The work was at the rear part of the Main engine room parts compartment, being the forward bulkhead of the Lucky Bag. The heat from welding or cutting convected through the thin bulkhead metal.

I was told by several ship mates that the skipper, and I don't know which one, Captain Wilson or Captain Outten that the **minor accident** he had with the ship at one time the **fire** and the **ship running aground** was not recorded in the ships log. If this were true there would be no record of it in the ships log?

If my life depended on the time of the fire during my tour of duty from October of 1952 through July of 1956 I could not remember. I personally asked Capt. Outten if he remembered the fire and he said NO.

That is why I am writing any ship mate who might have remembered these events and if do remember it, if they could or would write me a letter about what you knew about it these events and allow me to forward this to the VA.

I am hoping someone will remember this because this fire almost killed me. I have dreams about it all the time. I am now suffering from PTSD, depression and have to take medication for depression and medication to sleep. I have been taking this medication for about a year and it does help. Before I received help from the VA I would awaken at night sometimes at two or three am and couldn't go back to sleep. I lived with this for about ten years. I was getting desperate and even considered suicide.

The VA also stated that the ship did not run aground on July 5th, 1953 in the Pusan Korea harbor. The VA said that the running aground was not in the ships log as well as the fire. The ship started to drag anchor when the storm came up. I know this to be fact because I had to enter the stern void tank and examine the size of the puncture and report to the Captain, via the engineering officer. Everyone on the ship was up all that night at special sea detail; during this time I was throttle man in the main engine room. I answered over 300 (bell changes) (forward and backward and high and low speeds) to avoid running aground. It happened the same night that the SS Cornhusker/Mariner ran aground, broke in half and sank, she was on her maiden voyage. I have pictures of that. The reason I wrote a stressor letter on this issue is because of the darkness in the tank, the water gurgling up, the terrible smell and slime. I have had since this incident for 50 years terrible feelings of entrapment; I cannot even go to movies because of darkness. I feel that this had enhanced my PTSD and depression that I am suffering now. I would also hope that someone might remember this happening.

If the fire, minor accident and the ship running aground, was not logged, I wonder how much information may not have been logged? I am requiring help on this if you do remember. I would love to hear from you.

I am thanking you and would greatly appreciate any comments should you have any.

My Home Phone number 816 587 5757
My Cell Phone number is 816 805 1266
Home address: 8218 N Revere Court, Kansas City, Mo 64151

13 April 2004

To Whom It May Concern

My name is Herman Harold Overton, I served in the U.S Navy from July 16th 1952 until August 1st 1956. My service number was 438 99 58. I enlisted in St. Louis Mo. and I went to Boot Camp at the Naval Training Center in San Diego, CA. After Boot Camp I was assigned to the LST1122, where I served until about January 1956 at which time I transferred to the USS Pickaway APA 222.

    During my time on the LST I became an electricians mate in the engineering department. It was my good fortune to become a close friend with an engineman by the name of Major Thomas I say that is was my good fortune because I had never met a finer person in my young life and to this day I don"t think I have ever met a finer person.

    Major was one of those people that always seemed to be where things needed to be done. Not only in his regular duties as an engineman but many other activities as well.

    The LST was sent to Japan/Korea in January 1953 where, until the war ended in August we ferried food, ammunition, guns, trucks, tanks and aircraft fuel to guerilla fighters fighting from the islands off the coast of Korea and to Pusan and Inchon carrying regular Army and Marine troops.

    I remember that one of Majors General Quarters assignments was to man an LCVP((LandingCraft Vehicle Personnel) during landing operations. He and I being pretty good friends (and both being from Missouri) kind of watched out for each other. I remember that he spent a lot of time in the LCVP'S, nicknamed Peter boats, During our operations that winter, and I think the winter of 1952 was the coldest weather I had ever experienced, it seemed that Major was always on the water. The Peter boats had no cover and all personnel aboard it were subjected to the worst of the cold elements. In addition to the cold weather when you added snow and rain it became the worst duty on the ship. Major never complained about serving on the Peter boats only that I remember him saying that he never seemed to be able to keep his feet dry or warm. It is understandable that Major is experiencing difficulties with his feet and toes. He has lost toenails; he cannot feel cold, hot or wet feet unless he feels them with his hands. He also reports a severe " burning" sensation in his toes and feet.

    I also remember Major and other boat crewmembers expressing their fears and anxieties when having to "beach" the islands in preparation for the ship to hit the beach. The contact had to be made with a ships officer in order to determine if the island was held by our forces and not the North Koreans or Chinese. The boat crews were not sure what might be waiting for them especially during nighttime operations.

    Of course being an engineman put his " underway duties " in the main engine room. Those diesel engines not only made a lot of engine noise but they seemed to emit a shrill scream. I remember having to go on watch at midnight in the auxiliary engine room where the diesel generators were at the same time that Major was going on watch in the main engine room. The hatches were just one compartment apart and when he opened the hatch to the main engine room I thanked my lucky stars that I didn't have to stand watch down there. The noise was deafening. I am not surprise that Major(and probably many other ex enginemen) now has severe problems with (tinnitus), ringing in the ears and other problems with his hearing loss.

Through the years I lost contact with Major and just recently became reacquainted as we are preparing to have a ships reunion of the LST crewmembers of 1952 to 1956.

He told me of the problems he has been having through the years and asked if I remembered his activities during our cruise together. Because the conditions were so severe back then I still remembered vividly about the ships activities and Majors role in particular. He asked me if I would write a letter describing some of the things that I remembered about his activities.

Respectfully

Herman Harold Overton

Herman Harold Overton
10929 Chardonnay Place
San Diego, Ca. 92131
(858) 693 0543

The above letter (previous 2 pages) is from Harold Overton who helped me to prove about my hearing problem and my dead feet from frost bite,

Major Thomas

This letter is from Don Ashworth who was a Radioman.

Donald W. Ashworth
2289 Cedar Lake Driver
Loganville, Ga 30052

February 6, 2005

To Whomever it may concern:

I was in the U.S. Navy from 1952 until 1955. Most of my service time was spent on the LST 1122. During a portion of my stint, Mr. Major Thomas served aboard the same ship in the engineering division.

My "rack" (sleeping quarters) was in the forward most compartment on the port (left) side. In order to get to my quarters, I had to travel the entire port side; proceeding through two rest room areas and several sleeping quarters.

On one occasion, going to my compartment or traveling away from my sleeping quarters I encountered several engineers, at least one officer, a chief and two or three other individuals congregated around a hatch from which smoke was billowing. Major Thomas was getting into an OBA (oxygen breathing apparatus). **(In boot camp, we had been required to put on an OBA and walk into a burning and smoke filled building and I recalled how harrowing an experience it had been. I empathized with the guy getting ready to enter that compartment.)** I watched as Major entered the smoked filled area. I remember standing around for a few minutes until an officer or the chief ordered us to leave if we had no involvement with the fire.

I recall proceeding to the radio shack, where I related to the folks on duty what I had observed.

Some time later, I passed through the area where the fire had occurred and observed burned mattresses and or sea bags. The damaged articles could have been other than those listed here; however, I do recall the damaged cargo as badly burned and charred. I believe it was still smoldering.

I have looked in my diary for the dates but have not located the particular diary on whic I had made notes. I will continue to research. Incidentally, I have a bundle of letters I had written my mother during my service time. I feel certain those letters are stored away some place. In those letters I feel sure I mentioned the fire. I will continue to search for those letters.

Regarding dragging anchor in Pusan Harbor, I clearly recall the incident, but do not have diary notes to verify times. My recollection is simply that a typhoon was brewing at sea. We had begun to drag anchor in the harbor. General quarters was sounded and we prepared to get underway. I do recall that we had difficulty leaving port. The reasons fo

& Life Goes On...

delay do not come to mind at this time. Possibly other ships were also leaving the harbor and we were waiting our turn.

Major says there was a merchant ship or cargo ship in the harbor which broke up and sank. I don't recall that part of it because I was probably on watch in the radio shack and unaware of other things taking place. For your information, radio traffic in times of stress, while serving in a war zone, is extremely heavy allowing no time to deal with other activities inside or outside of the ship. Morse code channels, voice circuits and teletype messages consume all of a person's attention.

I hope this is helpful. In the event I find my letters and diary, I will forward copies to Major Thomas.

Sincerely,

Donald W. Ashworth

Phone no. 770 466 2209
Email dashworth415@cs.com

Major Thomas

02-09-05

To Whom This May Concern

This letter is in regard to Major Thomas' request about the fire in the Lucky Bag Compartment on the LST 1122. I know there was a fire because I had to inspect when I returned from being on liberty. I know this is true because I was restricted ship for two weeks having a non-certified standby that day for liberty. Major Thomas was my stand by and he was not certified for use of the OBA.

I had to have classes for the ships crew on operating an OBA (oxygen breathing apparatus). Since I was not aboard the ship when the fire occurred Major was filling for me and was the one that had to try and put out the fire and save the LST 1122.

This is all the information that I have concerning the fire.

I served aboard the LST 1122 from 1951-*1954.

      Richard L. Burmood

      1111 West 40th Street

      Kearney, Nebraska 68845

Service # 318-7383

& Life Goes On...

A-Ship Apparently in Japan in Mid-'60s

By Rudy Maxa and
Washington Post Staff Writer; Staff writer Morton Mintz contributed to this article.
June 3, 1981

A U.S. Navy ship apparently carrying nuclear weapons remained off the coast of Japan into the mid-1960s, at least three years after senior officials in the Kennedy administration have said they understood the Pentagon had ordered it to stay clear of Japanese territory.

The USS San Joaquin County, an LST (landing ship, tank), remained 100 to 200 yards offshore from the Marine air base at Iwakuni through 1964 and perhaps later, according to two officers who were stationed on the ship.

The presence of a vessel with a cargo of neclear weapons violated a mutual security treaty that forbade the United States to deploy nuclear weapons in Japanese territory.

When I was building the garage at our Lake house, I was called by one of the rating board employees at the St. Louis VA headquarters. They told me that I was considered unemployable due to the condition of my damaged feet.

On February 19, 2005, the VA made a final decision, I was rated as non-employable. I cannot work for wages ever again. Fine with me. I am considered 100% disabled.

Their decision helped Erna get her prescriptions through the VA. That helped a lot with our prescription expenses.

Chapter Fifteen

Back to Civilian Life

Is there life after serving for four years in the Navy active duty? Yes! On July 11, 1956 I received an honorable discharge from the U.S. Navy at Treasure Island, San Francisco, California.

I arrived in Jefferson City, Missouri on July 13, 1956 and hitchhiked home to Owensville to surprise my parents and siblings a few days before my expected arrival date.

With help from Dad, we purchased a new Ford truck in Hermann, Missouri. We transported livestock from the Owensville area to stockyards in St. Louis and East St. Louis.

Major
Truck for Hauling

I transported livestock at night and worked as a truck driver and truck/ tractor mechanic during the day. Sometimes I would make two trips to St. Louis with livestock at night getting home just in time to clean up and go to work at the local MFA (Missouri Farmers Association) the next morning.

I welded parts brought in by customers that needed fixing like John Deere farm implements and chain saws. I made service calls to farms to make repairs to farm machinery, cream separators, and fix anything else that my boss Fred Koenig thought I could repair.

Chapter Sixteen

Erna and Me

When I got out of the Navy, I made a pledge that I was not going to get married. I worked 10-15 hours a day, as a mechanic at a MFA in Owensville. I bought a new Ford truck and hauled livestock at night.

On April 1, 1957, my brother Eldred asked me to go out with him and his girlfriend to a movie. I reluctantly went. However, it was one the most important days of my life. I met a sweet girl and I fell in love immediately.

My sister was there waiting for the movie to start. She came up and asked if I wanted a date. At first I said no, but she got a friend of hers, Erna Schmidt as a date for me.

Erna and I sat through the movie and visited. After the movie, we went to the local kids hang out and had a coke or something and then I took her to her grandmother's house in Owensville. We started dating and it got to be a very serious relationship.

Erna went to St. Louis, to obtain a job as per her parent's expectations, after she graduated from high school. I followed her. Erna found a job at Mercantile Bank.

I obtained a job with the St. Louis Public Transit System. I was one of 13 mechanics they hired for winter work. I worked the second shift checking 150 busses every night to make sure they didn't freeze up. They didn't use antifreeze at that time, so the engines were left running all night,.

I felt the heater piping through the side window and the pipes had to be warm. If not, I took them to the barn to thaw them out.

At the end of winter 1957, I was laid off at the St. Louis Public Transit Company. I was one of thirteen to be laid off and I was number thirteen on the seniority list. This was a normal cut back procedure.

Through Erna, I found out I was adopted. What a shock! I took Erna with me to confront my mother about this.

"I can't imagine who would start a rumor like that anyway," was the first think she said. Well I got a little uptight because I should have known about this a long time ago.

She finally admitted I was adopted and told me to never tell Dad because it would kill him if he knew that I knew about my adoption.

In October of 1957, I purchased an engagement ring. I went to Erna's parents and asked for her hand in marriage. They both shared their blessings. Then I drove to St. Louis, where Erna was staying and proposed to her that evening.

She said yes!

Thank you God.

June 7, 1958 was our wedding day. It was very hot, and there was no air conditioning at the church or at Erna's home. We were married at Wollam St. Johns United Church of Christ.

The Rev Herbert Baur Pastor of St. Peters UCC in Owensville, Missouri officiated. The wedding was at 6:00PM. The reception was at Erna's parents' home. Afterwards, the neighbors held a chivaree.

I had obtained a job with the United Motor Exchange, they gave me two days for our honeymoon. Shortly after that in 1958, I went to work for Delmar Motors.

In 1991, after Pamela and Cynthia were married and on their own, Erna and I hit another rough spot. But my best friend and I met it together.

Erna found out that her mammogram showed positive for cancer in her right breast. Breast cancer. She had to have a radical mastectomy. She was lucky though, the cancer didn't spread anywhere else. She didn't have to do chemo, but she took Tomoxifin for five years.

Nine years later in 2000, Erna was diagnosed again with cancer in her left breast. I was in a transition period between being laid off at Butler Transport and getting a job at Midwest. Lucky enough, the insurance I had at Butler was still in effect.

First, she had exploratory surgery to verify the mammogram findings: the surgery verified the cancer. The biopsy surgery was in January. It was cold, with a lot of snow. The surgery was scheduled very early in the morning and the snow was beginning to worry us.

We both thought about going to a hotel close to Liberty Hospital in Liberty, Missouri. But we didn't. Instead, we got up real early and started out. The streets and highways were not treated or plowed. The snow was already about six inches deep. There were autos in ditches and in the medians. It was really becoming a treacherous drive. We wondered if the surgeon would make it.

After we got to the hospital, Erna was prepped for surgery. The surgery went okay, but the recovery from the anesthetic was another story. I waited for a good hour before I heard anything about the surgery or recovery. Finally the doctor came to the waiting room and told me he couldn't wait for Erna to wake up any longer: he had other surgeries that morning. So I asked him what the biopsy revealed. He said it was cancer. God, what a blow to me. I was going to have to tell Erna.

I went into the recovery room where they were having a very difficult time getting Erna to come out of the anesthetic. I saw the nurses prop her up in the bed and then she started coming around. She saw me and I came to the bedside. The first thing, she asked was, "What did the doctor say?"

I almost broke down when I told her it was cancer. That was one of the most difficult and painful things I ever had to do in my entire life. Then she responded, well we went through it once, we can do it again.

Little did she know it was going to be much more difficult because she was going to have to do chemotherapy, which almost killed her.

Erna had to decide if she wanted another surgery for removal of the left breast or just complete the chemo. Her rationalization was if the breast were removed, she wouldn't have the threat of more breast cancer. She opted for the surgery.

During the operation two lymph nodes were removed for a pathology test to see if the cancer had spread. Well it did. So, she had yet another surgery to install a Groshon catheter for receiving the chemotherapy and other medical injections to her blood stream. (She had lymphedema in her arms and needles could not be used.)

Next came the terrible, devastating, immobilizing chemotherapy. It was a long, drawn out treatment which pretty well consumed the year of 2001. Erna was in the hospital eight times that year. She would get deathly ill. Her blood was so thin that the doctors didn't want her to brush her teeth for fear that if the gums started bleeding, it could not be stopped. She struggled through it and remained cancer free. Hurray for my best friend!

While I was caring for Erna during her chemotherapy, I was driving a truck for John's Delivery. I started to work on getting the cabin at the lake torn down and readying the place so we could put up 60' x 30' modular home.

But before I really got into working on the lake project, depression had me so down that I was going to sell the lake property. I was so deep in the depression that I didn't want to do anything. I told Cindy I was going to sell the property and she kept trying to talk me out of it.

But soon afterwards, the medication started helping me to get back on track. I also got some medication to help me sleep that worked for a year or so. But recently, I've had to use a different medication, and more of it.

Due to Erna's illnesses, we couldn't get to the lake very much for several years. We didn't have the time, Erna couldn't make the trips and we also were watching our finances closely. The place just sat there and deteriorated as the years went by.

I hadn't run my boat with the new outboard engine since we'd moved back to Kansas City. From 1991 through 2004 we just didn't have the time. With Erna suffering from the residuals of chemotherapy and other illnesses, we just didn't make it to the lake much.

Jim and Cindy purchased a place across the cove where our cabin was. They worked on it constantly for seven or eight years and made a mansion of it. Jim built several other buildings across the road from their mansion: two boat storage buildings, a small shop and later a wood working shop. He also built a large building he transformed into a shop large enough to house a hydraulic vehicle hoist. He was preparing for his retirement years.

In 1993, we gave thanks to Cindy and Jim for helping to finance a trip for us to go to an LST Reunion in Las Vegas. We had a great time! The WW2 LST guys really didn't want anything to do with Korean era vets. So, that would be my first and last reunion with the National LST Association.

But in May 2002, we held our first LST 1122 reunion in Omaha, Nebraska. It was great to see shipmates that I hadn't seen for 50 Years

The second ship reunion was held in Grapevine, Texas. Again, it was in the first part of May, 2003.

In May 2004, the third reunion was held in Mobile, Alabama. We flew to Mobil and rented a car. We stayed there for about four days

During the year 2004, I really started having problems. I couldn't sleep. Many, many nights I laid in bed, rolling and tossing: but no sleep.

The ringing in my ears tormented me. If I was sleeping, the ringing in the ears awakened me. I would cry at the drop of a hat at any little thing. Then, I would have to get up the next morning and go drive a truck, with no sleep. I did that off and on for a couple of years.

Finally, I started going to the VA hospital for tests and evaluation for depression. The doctors there diagnosed me with Post Traumatic Stress Disorder (PTSD). I started seeing a psychologist and a psychiatrist. The psychiatrist diagnosed me with deep depression with suicidal tendencies.

She started me on two different pills. It just so happened we were leaving the next week for St. Louis to attend my ship's reunion. I told her I was planning the trip. She told me I wasn't going anywhere unless I saw her before going. She said she had to know how the medication was doing.

Major Thomas

When I told her I was going to go, she said, very strongly, that if I didn't see her before going, she would have me committed. I had the feeling that she wasn't kidding, so I visited her before going to St. Louis, for the LST 1122 fourth annual reunion.

Erna and I attended as many ship reunions as we could. The 6th reunion was in Branson, Missouri, the 8th reunion was in Austin, Texas and 9th reunion was Oklahoma City. Erna loved the ship reunions, a high light in her life. She was loved by all the Navy veterans and their spouses.

In 2009, there was a ship reunion coming up Laughlin, Nevada. It was a long trip, but we stayed in Amarillo, Texas on the way. The second night we stayed in Albuquerque, New Mexico. We arrived in Laughlin in the next afternoon. Daughter Pam met us in Laughlin and spent several days with us.

The reunion people there had already set up a day trip to Oatman, Arizona. Oatman was a few miles from Laughlin so we drove several cars to get there. The week before we went to Oatman, the little town had hosted a group of bikers. A good size herd of Donkeys lived in the area and liked to come to Oatman for handouts.

Well the townspeople feared the bikers would be rude with the donkeys so the donkeys were driven out of town for that week to keep them safe. At the gift shops, they sold little bags of carrots to hand out to the donkeys.

The donkeys were sullen and would block the road into Oatman, then we'd have to wait until they decided to let us through. But we enjoyed the day. We had a lunch and after potty stops, we decided to head back to Laughlin.

On the way out the donkeys blocked the road. They came up alongside the car and stuck their heads in through the car windows begging for carrots. What a nasty mess! The donkeys drooled all over Erna's hand getting the carrots out of the bag. Erna wasn't too happy about that.

The next day we took a jet boat ride to Lake Havasu to see the London Bridge. Erna wanted to go so bad but was very worried about whether she could get aboard the jet boat. We had plenty of help getting her on board. We enjoyed the boat ride and when we arrived at Lake Havasu, we toured the London Bridge and the little shops in the area. We got Erna back on board and headed for Laughlin. That ship reunion there was one of our favorite reunions.

At our ship reunion in Austin, Texas, we took a side trip to Fredericksburg, Texas. The home of Admiral Nimitiz. We toured several museums there.

Erna and I joined the Kent Memorial Lutherans Church in Sunrise Beach, Missouri, Lake of the Ozarks, early spring, 2008.

We attended the Festival of Sharing event on October 17-18, 2010. The Festival of Sharing is a yearly event, dating many years back.

Quilts are made by parishioners throughout the state, then donated to the Festival of Sharing to be auctioned off. For every five dollars of money taken in at the Auction, a blanket is purchased for the needy throughout the world.

Erna bid on quilts and mainly crib quilts so she could give them to family members having babies. She would then send them to members of our family.

Our 50th wedding celebration was celebrated at the Wenwood Farm Winery on June 1, 2008. Wenwood is a neighboring farm to our family farm. It was originally a dairy farm for many years. The Neese family (owners of the farm) discontinued the dairy operation and started a winery which has been a great success.

Because most of the family would be together during the spring fling in May, we knew it would be more convenient to celebrate our 50th anniversary then. It was a success!

Many friends and family members attended. We had wine bottled with a picture of us on the label. We had friends and relatives help us make the food for the celebration.

We went back home at the Lake of the Ozarks (Ivy Bend area). A few days later we went to Lake Ozark to Baxter's Restaurant to have a nice meal and celebrate our anniversary. It was a precious time.

& Life Goes On...

Erna and Me
50th Wedding Dinner
At the Lake

★★★★★★★★★

In 2010, Erna was very involved with the Owensville High School Reunion. Her class was the host class. We attended the event from August 8-10 that year and were involved with all aspects of the event.

Chapter Seventeen

Our Family

July 12th 1959, Cynthia Renee Thomas was born. We lived at 4366 West Pine Blvd in St. Louis where we managed an apartment building. We didn't have to pay much rent so we were able to purchase some new furniture. Cindy's birth day was very hot. Missouri Baptist hospital was not air conditioned, and neither was our apartment. But we survivied. We paid $20.00 per week rent, and had just enough for groceries.

We went to Sears right after Cindy was born and made a huge purchase, we bought a twin blade window fan. We really had to sacrifice to get that fan.

I found a job with the American Bakeries Co. as mechanic. Finally I got health insurance and benefits. I started driving eighteen-wheelers while working for them. Drivers would call in sick and I took their runs. Over the 30 years I worked for American Bakeries, I drove approximately one million miles in eighteen-wheelers, bobtails and route vans.

In December 1961, American Bakeries Co in St. Louis transferred me to the Kansas City plant to work as Fleet Manager. Kansas City had 58 inches of snow that year. I dug out trucks that were stuck in deep drifts everywhere.

Erna was pregnant and supposed to deliver in March. We planned to take Cindy to Grandma's so Erna wouldn't have to be taking care of Cynthia during the delivery time.

Just when I was getting Cindy in the car to leave, Erna started crying. It just broke my heart. I arrived at Grandma's around midnight and woke them up.

Grandma offered to come to Kansas City to help out. I jumped at the chance. We arrived back in Kansas City around daybreak. Erna so happy to see Cynthia and her mom. I felt so much better for her.

The final move to Kansas City from St. Louis was on New Year's Eve, 1962. We arrived in Kansas City around midnight. I wasn't familiar with the city at all, I'd only been working there for a couple of weeks. But I did remember how to get to the bakery.

From there I was able to get us to our new apartment in the north part of Kansas City. The apartment was in one of two new apartment complexes north of the river.

March 26th 1962, found us at the St. Mary's Hospital, for the arrival of Pamela Dawn Thomas. It was a beautiful morning: air was crisp and skies were clear and blue. What a beautiful day to enter the world. I was so pleased with the new arrival and with Erna who had given her life. Thank you God.

Pam broke her right elbow and was in traction at the North Kansas City hospital for three weeks. That was an episode. She was about 3 or 4 years old.

We purchased our first house, I was able to take advantage of the VA for a loan. We paid $14,500 for it. The split level house had a one car garage. That fall, we finally purchased a second vehicle.

My adoptive father, Major Thomas Sr. passed away, February 12th, 1968. He was 63.

Major Thomas

Erna worked at the Park Hill School District as a clerk and letter writer for the higher-ups. She could mess up a computer at the drop of a hat. She kept the computer guy busy all the time.

But she was well loved by all and they took care of her. If she was walking to the printer, if she would be walking out to the parking lot, they were always there to help her.

Somehow, she got interested in making up and dressing small teddy bears and other little critters to give to the Salvation Army. Then the Army distributed the little critters to children around the city. In memory of Erna, the program is still ongoing.

Erna had to have a hysterectomy in June of 1983. It was a very difficult and painful time for her. I stayed in town the week she was to go to the doctor's office and have the stitches removed. She was in a tremendous amount of pain for several days before going to the doctor's office. We both sensed something was wrong.

She had a very painful walk from the house to the car, with every bump I hit, she felt severe pain. It was a struggle for her to get into the doctor's office but she finally made it. After we were there for a while, they took her to a room where they were to take the stitches out.

She wasn't in there very long when all hell broke loose. The nurses were running around with towels, hustling around and talking very low. I knew something was not right. A few moments later, a nurse came to tell me Erna was going to have to go back into surgery. She'd actually come apart at the incision.

They had her on a gurney and we rolled her across the parking lot to the hospital. She went into surgery almost immediately. After surgery the surgeon came to me and said that 'we' used wire this time so she should be okay. I asked him why he didn't use wire the first time so Erna wouldn't have had to go through surgery again. He made no comment. I think he was afraid we might sue, but we didn't.

Cindy attended Maple Woods College, 1977 through 1978 and studied Psychology and Interior Design.

In September 1980, we purchased a property at the Lake of the Ozarks, It has a run-down cabin on it. We worked on the cabin for years thereafter. We finally got it to be quite comfortable and enjoyed it over the years.

Pam started college in Warrensburg, MO. Central Missouri State College. She started the same year we purchased the lake property in 1980. She graduated from CSMU in 1984. She completed her internship at St. Louis University in 1985. Then she struck out for Dallas, Texas to seek her fame and fortune

Sometime in the mid 1970's, I bought a 1954 Ford bread truck and completely rebuilt it. I put new tires on it and installed an air conditioner.

The engine and transmission were not in the truck, so I bought a Chevrolet engine and transmission and installed them. I installed a table to eat from and put in a bed for night.

We drove it all over the upper midwest mountains. It ran well with no problems.

Camping in the Rockies
Erna, Major & Pam

& Life Goes On...

When Pam was getting close to driving age, I had a friend who was a truck tire salesman. He had a 1969 GTO Pontiac with no engine or transmission. He wanted a pool table I had so we traded the GTO for the pool table.

I put a new Chevrolet 6-cylinder engine and a Chevrolet transmission (automatic) in it. I gave it to Pam for her sixteenth birthday.

She was so excited to drive it, she drove it all the way through college, her internship in St. Louis and to Texas to work. She had it in Texas for several years. It never gave her any trouble. But then, some jerk rear-ended her and that was the end of the GTO.

Daughter Pamela got married to Ric Church at Cooper Hill, Missouri. The church setting was just beautiful. Cooper Hill is a very small community nestled in the pines on a small hill.

Pamela was a very pretty bride. Their marriage day was October 24th 1987. The trees were in full color. We drove up from Monroe, Louisiana for the wedding, but had to quickly return for our jobs.

Pam had a very demanding job as a registered dietician. She was living and working in Seal Beach, California. Ric kept busy with stress management classes and lectures all over the country.

When they were first married, they lived in Dallas but in 1989 or 1990, they moved to Seal Beach, California. That was their permanent home.

Daughter Cynthia married Jim Smith February 1988 at the church we had attended for years: Bethel United Church of Christ located in the northern part of Kansas City.

Major Thomas

The wedding was beautiful. Cindy was a very pretty bride. We drove up for the wedding from Monroe, Louisiana. We could only stay for a few days before we needed to return to our jobs. If I remember correctly they went to Hawaii for their honeymoon.

Cynthia worked for Federal Express and was with them over 25 years. Her job required a lot of extra time and effort. She went through different computer classes to improve the company's performance.

After living in Louisiana for about 4 years, we decided we were going to be just like them if we stayed there. We decided to sell out and head for Kansas City.

Gene Ridder, Erna's brother in law and Steve Smith came to Louisiana to help us move. We moved into a very nice apartment called Walnut Grove.

I got a job with Butler Transport and had worked there for about a year when Erna's mother passed away. I took three days off to help Erna and her family in their time of need. When I came back, I was terminated for taking those three days off.

Still through it all, we hunted for a home we could call our own. In the spring of 1992, we moved into 8218 N. Revere Court. It was a town house near the airport in north Kansas City.

My 70th birthday was coming up, so Cindy and Jim came to help celebrate. Then Pam and Ric came from California to help celebrate. Cindy and Pam worked hard by helping to make it successful.

That night Jim, Cindy, Pam, Ric, Erna and I went out to a very nice restaurant in Riverside, called Piropos, it was elegant dining.

& Life Goes On...

Our Family
At Major's 70th Birthday
2004
Pam, Me, Cindy, Ric, Erna, Jim

The following day we went to have a family portrait made. It was a very special birthday celebration. We ordered food catered. What food was left over we took to homeless shelter in Kansas City.

Erna and I got tired of accumulating rent receipts so we decided to hunt for a home we could purchase. We looked for a few months and found a new townhouse in north Kansas City near the airport.

We liked the area and the house: inside and out. So we purchased it. We moved into the new home towards the end of the summer of 1992.

We lived there until we sold it in 2005 to move to our new modular home at the Lake of the Ozarks when we retired.

In 2005, I began diligently packing to prepare for moving to the cabin at the Lake of the Ozarks. We put some items in storage or aside for a garage sale. I started earnestly preparing to put our Kansas City house on the market.

I packed and hauled stuff to the storage place near our lake property. I obtained the construction loan that we'd need for the installation of the modular home. I located a reputable contractor to get the foundation dug for the 60-foot basement. I was still driving for Johns' delivery as I could.

Our lake neighbors Wayne and Sally, allowed me to stay in their home when I was at the lake working so I wouldn't have to go all the way to Laurie, which is a small town about twenty miles from the Lake, to get a motel there. They both took very good care of me. They helped all they could. I couldn't have done it without their help.

I lined up a company to drill the well, and a company to do the concrete work. We ran electricity from the power pole to the basement so we would be ready to set the modular on and hook up the water and electricity.

Looking back today, I wonder how I got it all done: building at the Lake and preparing the house in Kansas City to sell. The house sold in late February and the person buying it was patient enough to allow us to stay there until we moved.

The modular was to be set the week after Memorial Day, but that didn't happen. It arrived three days late. The crew set it up, moved it to the basement foundation and got it all prepared for living.

When the modular arrived, water had gotten into the master bedroom ceiling and the drywall fell down which damaged the carpet. That all had to be repaired and new carpeting was installed.

The dates were set for the closing on the house in Kansas City and moving. We closed on June 2nd, and moved the next day. Erna's brother Glen, her sister Gloria, and Gloria's husband Gene came to Kansas City to help us move.

I made arrangements for a rental truck three weeks before the move. All was planned. We moved in, even with no carpet in master bedroom and the air conditioning not on-site or hooked up.

It rained all that day so mud was a problem. Because of all the construction around the building, there was no grass. Erna fell while we were moving in, twisting her ankle and leg which added to her problems.

We went to the storage building and brought one truckload of furniture I had hauled there about a month before. Son in law Jim made the steps from the main floor to the basement. He and Wayne wired up the lights in the basement.

We slept in the guest bedroom for at least a month before the new carpet arrived and was installed. The air conditioner did not arrive until about same time. Thank God the outside temperatures were still not too bad. The modular was well insulated.

With our neighbors Wayne and Sally's help, we started building the garage. The floor was poured. We worked every day, even in temperatures reaching over 100 degrees. We started early in the morning and knocked off around noon. It was just too hot, especially when we did the roofing. It was so hot the shingles would stick together.

Building the garage took all of July and August. The first of September, I was carrying a ladder from the garage to the basement when I fell over the ladder and broke my right leg next to the ankle. That was really a step backwards.

I had to have an ambulance take me to Jefferson City; the ambulance company would not take me to the VA hospital like I wanted. I had surgery, at St. Mary's Hospital in Jefferson City, they put two screws in and I was grounded for two months.

Erna and I were fully retired and had been living full time at the Lake for over a year. We both loved it; we loved retirement. We could sleep as late as we wished and pick up and go whenever we want. Erna loved to do sewing, puzzles, dominos, and to sleep in.

Since we had moved permanently, we added a deck to the front of house and planted jillions of flowers. We made flowerbeds and purchased a golf cart. It made getting around the area a little easier than walking or driving a car or truck.

When winter 2007 iced us in, we worried if we might lose power, so we got a portable generator and installed a propane fireplace insert for emergencies.

I was voted into Ivy Bend Volunteer Fire Department as a board member. I served on the board while we lived at the Lake. I also repaired fire trucks. Ivy Bend has no tax base therefore no tax dollars come in to maintain the trucks, it's all volunteer work.

I was informed by Erna's brother in law that there was a 1944 John Deere tractor in Owensville for sale. I drove to look at it and was impressed. I bought it and brought it home to the Lake. I used it in the Ivy Bend-fest, parade, a yearly 'fest' that takes place second week of September. I also had a 1959 Allis Chalmers (CA) tractor. Both were in the parade, along with our golf cart.

My youngest brother Eldred, passed away in September 15, 2009, from complications of bladder cancer. I truly loved my brother. Eldred and I have many memories back to the times when we lived in Owensville, during our high school years. He and I worked on many projects on the farm, making new fences, building hog houses, cutting sprouts, cutting down trees.

Erna's father, Richard W. Schmidt, passed away in October 2004. He was a very successful farmer. He was born, raised and died on that same farm. His favorite job or pastime was cutting and splitting wood. He was doing just that when he passed away: he died doing what he loved to do. He was 92.

With the passing of Erna's father, Richard Schmidt, the family decided to plan work days to help maintain the farm for future generations. A 'spring fling' and 'fall fling' weekend would make it easiest for most family members to attend because the family was spread out in places like California and Chicago.

The Friday of each fling weekend would be the work day. Saturday would be the play day. Then after church on Sunday, all would head for their homes.

In May the farm fling was in full swing with lots of friends, relatives, as always a good time was had by all. Gloria always works so hard to see that all is going ok. Especially keeping track of all the grand kids.

We attended the St. Paul E& R church in a small village not far from the farm: Cooper Hill. I was asked by Erna's sister, Gloria to consider making a stained glass window for the entrance to the church.

Knowing Erna's sister as I do, she is a person who I have a difficult time saying No to.

Therefore I made a stained glass window and installed it at the church.

& Life Goes On...

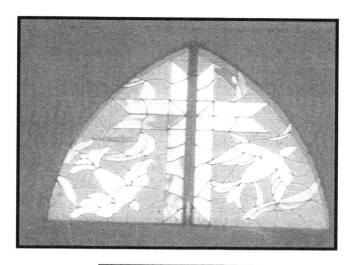

St. Paul's Cooper Hill Church

The Sunday the glass window was dedicated, we all attended St. Paul's Church in Cooper Hill. The Dedication Ceremony litany is shown on the next page.

Major Thomas

DEDICATION OF STAINED GLASS WINDOW

HYMN
"I Love to Tell the Story" .... Number 560

ADDRESS
Major Thomas, Creator

READING OF SCRIPTURE
Psalm 24

LITANY
Leader: For the glory of God's creation shown in the colors of this gift and for the doves of peace reflected in the beauty of this window.
People: We dedicate this stained-glass window at the entrance to God's peaceful presence and this sanctuary of faith.
Leader: For the cross of Jesus Christ depicted in this gift, which is central to our faith and for the glory of the cross which brings salvation to all people.
People: We dedicate this stained-glass window at the entrance to Christ's loving presence and this sanctuary of Christian fellowship.
Leader: For the flames of the Holy Spirit which encompass this window and is given to all who follow our Savior and for the strength it gives.
People: We dedicate this stained-glass window at the entrance to the Holy Spirit's working in this world and this sanctuary of Christian service.
Leader: For the skill and vision of Major Thomas, a servant of Jesus Christ and a friend of St. Paul's Church whose creativity is revealed in this gift.
People: We dedicate this stained-glass window at the entrance to the work and worship of this faith family and this sanctuary of sacramental ministry.
Leader: At this moment we dedicate this stained-glass window to the glory of God, to the honor of Jesus Christ, and to the praise of the Holy Spirit.
People: Thanks be to God!

PRAYER
O God of all creation, we give thanks for the calling to be your church and for the power you give us to fulfill our calling. We are a people with a past full of assurance and a future full of hope. Today we dedicate this stained-glass window to you. May the meaning we see in this gift of Major Thomas live on in us so that each time we see it we may be reminded of your holy presence. And may we pass on the significance of this gift to others. Amen.

The Reverend Charles Kurtz asked me if I would share with the congregation what symbols of the red, yellow and orange flames stood for, and what the white doves and cross represented.

So I informed the congregation about the assistance I obtained while planning and designing the window. I had a lady friend at the lake who heard I was starting a project for a church window.

She was married to a veteran who had served in England and went over there with him. She spent many hours visiting different churches and cathedral, always admiring the beautiful stained glass windows.

Somehow she got connected with someone at the Notre Dame Church and ended helping to design and free-hand draw some patterns for the windows. Her skills at free-hand drawing made my job much easier.

I had some professional help in the design and we spent many hours on it. We used up a couple of erasers until finally, we agreed. The design would be appropriate for St. Paul Church, Cooper Hill, Missouri.

For centuries faithful Christians observed with great devotion the Ascension of Jesus Christ. The Church celebrated Ascension Day on the fortieth day after Easter. It is always a weekday: Thursday.

Ascension is seen as the final act in God's drama of redemption and marks the completion of Christ's ministry on earth. The Easter season continues on corresponding with the length of time the disciples waited in Jerusalem for the gift of the Holy Spirit: Pentecost.

2009 was a great year for Cindy and Jim Smith! They finally got to retire full-time at the Lake. General Motors closed the dealership where Jim worked, so he retired.

Cindy was able to "shove it to 'em' in October. It worked out and they retired, retired, retired. They sold their home in Gladstone, Missouri and made the move.

Our niece Paige Ridder, got married to Chris Riegel in December 2009. We went to the wedding with the threat of snow following us all the way to St. Louis. We enjoyed the ceremony and reception. Then we headed for home in the snow.

Our nephew Chad was stationed in Kuwait, so he was unable to attend the wedding. He had to remain at his station for a few more months. We kept him in our prayers the whole time he was gone.

Chapter Eighteen

Work Life

I worked for American Bakeries for about 30 years. I was on call 24/7, three hundred, and sixty-five days a year. I worked in snowstorms and below zero temperatures. Sometimes, I worked 24 hours straight. Being in management, I traveled to cities like: Indianapolis, Cincinnati, St. Louis, and New York to work strikes. It wasn't a fun time.

I had dogs threaten me and knives and guns pulled on me. I drove trucks during those strikes, delivering products produced by management people from all over the country. I delivered product as far as Pennsylvania. I hauled flour to the plants because the Union drivers would not cross picket lines.

In the middle of the 1970's, I passed my first kidney stone. The first time was so painful and I wasn't sure what the pain was from. I was at work early that morning; I always was at work around 6AM.

I went to the bathroom and the urine was dark like coffee. I rationalized the reason for the dark color was because I was tired and so busy that my body just didn't process all the coffee I was drinking. Ha, was I in for a surprise. I was bleeding from the urinary tract. I started passing about two or three kidney stones a month.

In 1977, I couldn't pass a large stone so it had to be removed surgically. That was a tough surgery. Over the years, I've

& Life Goes On...

probably passed at least 300 stones. I still pass one once in a while but nothing like it was during the 1970's.

In the early 1970's, I drove for Consolidated Freightways for about a year. I pulled three trailers (joints) between Kansas City to Wichita, Kansas. It was a good company to work for with excellent pay and benefits. Then my kidney stones got worse and I had to quit driving.

In early 1971, I attended truck driving school at Braidwood, Illinois. I entered the school to learn about the new Federal Truck Driving Rules put out by the Interstate Commerce Commission (ICC).

These rules pertained to drivers' hours of service, break times and driver requirements that provided for closer inspections of vehicles. It was a good resource that helped me teach safety seminars for drivers.

The ICC was established in February 1889 to regulate trucking and railroads but in reality, it had very little control over trucking. The ICC was abolished January 1996. The Department of Transportation was established in April, 1967.

Consolidated Freightways
1971

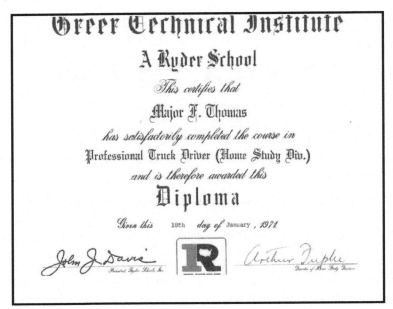

In the mid 1970', I was nominated to be a Mason by my friend, Jim Pirtle. After many hours of study and learning ritual, I was initiated as a third class Mason.

Then, I was nominated to become a Shriner. I attended a day long training to become a 32nd degree Scottish Rite and then was initiated as a Shriner.

The gas crisis in the mid 1970's prompted me to buy a little Cushman Motor Scooter that I drove to work when weather permitted.

& Life Goes On...

In the late 1970's and early 1980's, I started working for the corporate office in New York City. I worked for the newly-appointed Director of Transportation.

I remained in Kansas City because of its central location in the States. I traveled to many plants throughout the country. I conducted safety seminars, audited transport driver's logs and audited any records that fell under the requirements of the Department of Transportation: state and federal.

Erna would take me to the airport on Monday morning and I would return the following Friday (in most cases). However I would have to stay over and finish my work if it was necessary.

If that happened, Erna came to where I was working. Then on Sundays, we would take day trips around that area. Erna really enjoyed that. I worked in New York a lot. We would go to New Jersey and to upper New York State to sight see. In the fall, we enjoyed the fabulous colors along the Hudson River.

In the mid-1980s I worked for corporate office out of Charlotte, North Carolina. I worked all over the country, doing internal auditing of DOT driver's records and log books and teaching safety seminars for over the road (OTR) drivers and route van drivers.

My boss told me not to leave town for a couple of weeks over the Christmas and New Year's holidays. He wanted me to rebuild an old rusted-out and rotted-wood 1931 Ford delivery van, which was in very poor condition.

I had to remove all the wood, fenders and running boards. I started from the frame up, replacing all the wood, rusted out running boards and everything else.

All of the wood was full quarter red cedar. I had a very difficult time trying to find a lumber yard in Kansas City that carried red cedar, full quarter wood. Luckily, I finally found a supplier.

I found a woodworker to cut the rear fender radius and dovetail the half circle for the fender opening. I installed new running boards and a new carburetor. Then I fully sanded down the new metal on the running boards and all the new wood. After that, I primed it and painted it. Then came the new 'Tastee' decals.

The truck was then taken all over Kansas City to grocery stores. The bread plant made miniature bread loaves to give to customers for the advertisement. It took me three months to complete the full restoration.

Soon, the other bread plants wanted to use it to advertise at their local grocery stores. So I made a trailer to transport it around the country.

Tastee Model A Truck
1931 Ford

& Life Goes On...

In 1986, American Bakeries was sold to Metz Baking Company of Sioux City, Iowa. I had to change jobs or be transferred. My boss took steps to transfer me to Louisiana, to Cotton Bros. Baking Co. which was owned by Interstate Brands Co. of Kansas City. I was transferred to Monroe, Louisiana.

Interstate Brands took care of selling our home in Kansas City. We moved to Monroe in 1987. I was in management as the Fleet Maintenance Superintendent. Erna worked for the state College there. .

It was a different culture, and we soon learned the people were not trustworthy. The people we bought our house from, lied to us. The foundation was cracked and sinking. The house inspector lied about the condition of the furnace: it had a crack in the firebox. We almost died from the noxious fumes it emitted. We spent over four thousand dollars to have piers put under the foundation.

While working for American Bakeries as a Fleet Manager at the corporate office, I traveled all over the country: San Jose, Houston, St. Paul, New York, St. Louis and many other cities. The company had to deal with contracts the Union forced upon them.

So, Metz Baking Company bought out American Bakeries and I was transferred from Kansas City to Monroe, Louisiana in 1987. I managed a 192 truck fleet.

The Cotton Brothers Baking Company had agencies (thrift stores) scattered all over the states of Louisiana, Mississippi and Texas. I had to be in constant contact with all the mechanics from Vicksburg to Shreveport, every location.

After living in Monroe, Louisiana four years, Erna and I decided we wanted to get back to Missouri. Louisiana culture was quite a different way of living than we were used to. So, we put our house on the market, I got a job with Butler Transport in Kansas City and we moved back to Missouri in the summer of 1991.

In 1992, I got a job working for Midwest Service and Tow, as shop manager. We worked on customer vehicles: eighteen-wheelers and smaller trucks. I also maintained ten tow trucks, and that was a job in itself. They ran 24/7.

I worked hard, long hours at Midwest keeping the tow trucks running. On a Saturday afternoon I was working on a vehicle with a winch problem. While the winch was being rolled on the drum I was holding on to it very tightly so it wouldn't kink.

Something jerked and almost knocked me off my feet. I felt a sharp pain in my right side. I became nauseous so I went to my office and just sat down. I broke into a sweat and was really hurting. I knew I had a hernia.

After work I went home and told Erna. On Monday morning, I went to work as usual. I told my boss about it and of course he wasn't too happy about it. He told me as soon as it was eight o'clock, I should go the clinic his company used for accidents and injuries.

At the clinic, I waited for quite some time for the doctor to come in the room. He walked in, put both hands up to his head and said you're supposed to have a hernia. I supposed he was talking to himself. What do I do now?

The doctor told me to take off all my clothes and lie on the table. He felt around my groin area and stomach. He said I didn't have a hernia. Well I knew I had one. I went back to the shop and told my boss what had happened. He asked if I wanted to get a second opinion and I said yes. I got in touch with a surgeon's group I had used in the past.

The surgeon had me stand and held his fingers at the groin area and had me cough. No doubt, I had a hernia. He suggested I make an appointment for surgery as soon as possible. I had the surgery and all went well. I was told by the doctor not to drive for two weeks. So I was out of circulation for about three weeks.

After returning to work, Mr. Sam, the company owner was very hateful with me. He called me 'old man' and joked about me getting hurt. One morning around 6am he came in my office in a tirade, madder than hell about me not getting one of his tow trucks repaired. Well he didn't know I'd gotten it repaired the past evening before I went home. He just kept ranting and raving until I started shutting off my computer and unplugging all the components. I carried my computer out to the truck and said good-bye.

When I got home around noon that day, Pat Gemmer was there talking to Erna. Erna asked me what I was doing home so early. I told her I had quit my job. I know she wasn't too happy about that, but enough is enough.

I crossed paths with John Clampitt, who owned a small trucking company that catered mainly to printers and printing suppliers. I started driving for Johns Delivery part time. I usually worked 20 hours a week, but the pay was good.

His business started to increase so he wanted to get into the tractor-trailer hauling to improve the company's peformance and the bottom line. I helped get the first tractor and trailer for John's. Then I drove it because at the time, none of his drivers were qualified or had a Class A license.

I ended up teaching John how to drive a tractor-trailer so he could get his Class A license. He is no longer in the trucking business.

Chapter Nineteen

My Adoption

I struggled with the adoption thing throughout the 1970's and 1980's. I wrote to Mom several times, requesting answers to my questions, but it was to no avail.

A week or so before the Thomas clan gathered in St. Charles for my brother Gerald and his wife Norma's twenty fifth wedding anniversary celebration, I wrote my Mom asking her about my adoption. I never received any response. Mom and I got into a shouting match there, about the letter I'd just sent her. I was so angry, I got the children and Erna and we headed back to Kansas City. That's when I made up my mind to search for my biological parents.

With the help of my loving cousin, Helen Jean Meyer, I began my search. Helen did most of the legwork. She went to different libraries in St. Charles, Missouri and Union, Missouri and looked through old newspapers.

I wrote letters to Catholic Services in St. Louis. I received letters back with clues in them. During the mid-1980's, I was working on my search for my biological parents. As I said, some of the pages offered us clues. For instance, someone wrote on the back of one sheet 'John Wald', and then erased it. So Erna took a pencil and rubbed over the name, which made it easy to see: 'John Wald'. Like when you do a grave rubbing. It helped me a lot to finally learn my birth name. I wrote Jefferson City to the Bureau of Vital Statistics requesting any information I could get that would help me find out about adoptions and birth certificates.

It took Helen and me three years to find the facts. When I was born, my birth-mother was aged 36. Her name was Mary Walde and she was born in 1898. She lived in Neier, Missouri and had attended St. Joseph Catholic School. She had worshiped at St. Joseph's Catholic Church. Mary Walde had died in March of 1952. She died the year I went into the Navy.

I visited her gravesite in Neier. I met some of my blood relations living in that area and they took me in. They told me stories about my mother. They talked about how she kept their family farm home so spotless. I talked to the person who nurtured her during her illness and her death. She gave me my birth-mother's kerosene lamp, and a few of her dishes. These type of dishes were the ones that local theaters gave away as promotional items. I feel that these things are the link between Mary and me.

Major Thomas

John Leo Walde AKA Major Thomas
St. Ann's Orphanage
Page and Union Blvds
St. Louis, Missouri
April 24th, 1934

I was born in St. Louis, Missouri at a Catholic orphanage that was at Page and Union Blvd. I was born on April 24th, 1934. I was named John Leo Walde named after my birth-mother's father, who had passed away before I was born.

From the orphanage, I was taken to a home of another couple, but the husband did not want me. I went back to the orphanage and was taken to the home of Major and Eva Thomas in July of 1935. I was officially adopted in August of 1936. I was baptized in the Catholic Orphanage at birth.

I found out through my birth-mother's family, who my father was. His name was Adolph Steve Seiss. He lived across the road from my birth-mother. He was a bit younger, age 19.

I talked to some of my birth-father's relations, his sisters. There were 11 siblings in that family. His sister, Florence lived in Florida. Steve lived in Clearwater, Florida. His sister Florence called Steve and told him about me and said that Steve would like to meet me.

So on a vacation that started out in Texas visiting Pam, Erna and I went on to Clearwater, Florida. We arrived at Steve's address but he was not home. We waited for a while and he finally arrived. He stopped me in the driveway and said that I couldn't be his son because he was sterile.

We talked face to face. Later Erna told me that our profiles were identical. But there we were. There were no more conversations with him. We went on and visited my Aunt Florence (Steve's sister) for a couple of days. She was getting up in the years. But many times she commented on how I looked so much like Steve. Steve had been in the Navy, and now wore a beard.

Steve was robbed and killed in Quitman, Mississippi sometimes in the late 1980's. He was on his way to visit relatives in St. Louis.

My adoptive mother, Eva Lillilan Mertle Thomas passed away, 11 days after September 11, 2001. She was 96. Her passing really threw me a curve ball. However much I loved her, she would not talk to me about the adoption. Never.

I wrote my mother dozens of letterS asking her to share the adoption matters with me, but she never did. I really was hurt. I kept hearing rumors about my adoption; such as my adoptive father's sister could have been my mother. Then I heard other rumors about the adoption until I had finally decided to search and find my birth parents.

My adoptive mother was my last link to ever finding out any more about the adoption. I feel this is when I really started into the deep depression. Helen Jean, my cousin buddy, told me to let it go. I have tried but I still have problems with it.

Chapter Twenty

Good Times!

This model of the LST 1122 is 6 inches wide, 41 inches long and 13 inches tall. It took me over a year to build it. Then I took it to our ship reunions all over the country.

In July 2011, I donated it to the Gasconade County Museum in Owensville, Missouri.

The model was greatly appreciated there at the Museum. I attended an ice cream social there and talked to the visitors about the model.

The picture below shows me explaining the LST 1122's ship functions.

I can't help feeling that some people think I am exaggerating my problems with depression and my not sleeping without medication. They don't know about the vivid flashbacks and memories of putting out the fire when I almost died.

I have not had many days for the past 60 years without having a flashback: day or night. They don't know the vivid flashback memories I have of the tense and fearful moments as we approached the islands where the ship was to beach and make contact with our people, and hopefully not the North Koreans or Chinese.

I have vivid flashbacks of the stinking, slimy, very dark tank I had to uncover, then enter to determine the damage in the bottom of the ship when it ran aground in Pusan, Korea. I still can hear the sound of water gurgling in that tank.

Even now, I have a terrible time with darkness, doors being blocked or being surrounded by other people. I thought it was claustrophobic.

The VA classifies this syndrome as Post Traumatic Stress Disorder (PTSD) The constant ringing in my ears until sometimes you just want to bang your head against the wall. You feel like you would do anything to stop the ringing.

The Thresher's show has been held at the Rosebud, Missouri Park for many years. We would take a tractor and the golf cart to the show so I could take Erna around the fair grounds. She would look at the different crafts that were displayed from vendors around the area.

I took my 1944 John Deere tractor to the Owensville Threshers show at Rosebud on the July 18-20, 2008. That was the first year I took the John Deere.

The specialty of the day was homemade ice cream. The ice cream was so popular that shortly after the ice cream was opened, the stand would be sold out.

We enjoyed watching the bale toss and the draft horses pulling sledges. They were so well trained. One couldn't help but feel sorry for them, they would work their hearts out to pull against each other in the heat.

Of course, my favorite mealtime sandwich was the fish sandwich, with a drink.

The Thresher's show is always in mid-July. There were several other shows throughout the years where the heat was almost unbearable. But we had a year or two when the weather was very tolerable.

& Life Goes On...

***Erna at the Thresher's Show
Rosebud, Missouri***

Erna loved the Thresher show each year we would take tractors, golf cart and a covered wagon, then spend a lot of time at the events. She loved to watch the horse teams pull, the hay bale toss, and the old time steam tractors. Of course she watched me drive my tractors at the parades.

At the Thresher's show in Rosebud on July 16-18, 2010, Pam came to visit and drove one of the tractors in the parade.

Major Thomas

Erna and I traveled to Sedalia, Missouri, north of Cole Camp. We found this old, beat-up trailer with flat tires.

We looked at each other and asked, "Why wouldn't that trailer work at parades with our old tractors?" So we bought it. My son in law Jim, helped me get it on my trailer to take home where I started rebuilding it.

I put all new wood on it: floor, side panels and stanchions before I put it back together. It had old horse-drawn tongues that I took apart before I rebuilt a new tongue to accommodate tractors. I gave the old tongues to a Mennonite harness maker and he was delighted with them. The tires were shot so I got new tires for it.

& Life Goes On...

As you can see, it looked pretty bad.

But progress was made. After I removed all the old rotted wood from the wagon, no wood was salvageable. I had to get all new wood from the frame up.

Major Thomas

The below picture is the finished product after I rebuilt the old wagon and made it into a Conestoga.. The wagon went to many parades.

Chapter Twenty One

Erna's Last Days on Earth

In 2010, Erna had to go to the hospital in Clinton, Missouri to get blood work, a bone scan and X-rays in preparation to an appointment with her Kansas City oncologist the coming week. When we got home the radiologist called to tell Erna she had pneumonia, which added to the rest of her health issues

While living at the Lake in our retirement, I usually got up earlier than Erna. The morning after the radiologist called, Erna tried to get out of bed and called to me. She couldn't sit up. She kept falling back down on the bed. I told her to put her arm down on the bed to hold herself up, which she did.

Then I called my son in law Jim to come over and help me. When I got back to the bedroom, Erna sitting up. "Come sit here by me, and don't you leave me." She said, looking up at me and patting the left side of the bed.

That alerted me that something was really wrong with her. I called 911. We lived about 30 miles from the closest town so it took almost 30 minutes for the paramedics to get there. The paramedics immediately checked her blood sugar. Sure enough it was low: 45.

In the days before, I'd been asking Erna if she'd tested her blood sugar. "Yeah..." she'd reply - in a bitchy way. But I never saw a syringe in the waste basket in the morning, so I suspected something was up. The paramedics gave her some glucose to bring her blood sugar back up and it worked.

"Well, Mrs. Thomas, your blood sugar is about up to normal so we will be getting ready to leave." The paramedics said.

"Not so fast." I said, "She just found out last evening that she has pneumonia. I want her to go to the hospital to help her get rid of the pneumonia."

So they transported Erna to St. Mary's in Jefferson City. After the phone call from Clinton Hospital I was really upset. I called Erna's primary care doctor whose office was in Versailles. I told her I wanted a prescription for Erna's pneumonia diagnosis. She hemmed around. Finally, I said, "if you don't have a prescription at Walmart now I will come up to your office and sit on your desk until I get it."

Walmart got the new prescription ready for me to pick it up. I wanted Erna to start the medications immediately so she would be healthy enough to go to Jackson, Mississippi in the spring time for our ship's reunion.

She was in the hospital for several days. The hospital and the insurance company were trying to get rid of her so a social worker at the hospital arranged to get Erna into Laurie Care Center.

The nurses said I couldn't take her by car because Erna had to be on oxygen. So I met her at the Laurie Care Center and got her situated in her room. We began planning and getting the care she needed.

In 2011, Erna, my wife of over 50 years, was still at the Laurie nursing home. I visited her every day and stayed most of the day with her. Her appetite improved, she was even getting her hair worked on.

On April 24th it was my birthday so Erna's sister Gloria and her husband Gene came to Laurie to visit. We went to Shrimp Daddy's for a noon meal, then went back to the Care Center. Cindy baked a pineapple upside-down birthday cake for me. We all shared the cake. Erna seemed to be feeling good as she visited with us.

The following week was pretty uneventful until Thursday. I arrived at the center around 9am. Two or three caretakers were trying to get Erna up, but she couldn't get up on her own. They got a lift machine so she could hold on handles as they lifted it up.

She barely got her weight off the bed before she started screaming, "I can't do it, let me down, let me down." They got her back down on the bed when she fell back almost cross ways in the bed. A caretaker got in the bed and another lifted Erna's legs up. Finally she was laying on the bed.

Within a few minutes Erna had a panic attack. She had trouble breathing, every breath was a lot of effort. She had oxygen, but it was still difficult to breathe. I sat holding her hand and watching her work hard for every breath.

I felt so sorry for her. I wished I could have done something to help her but I couldn't. Every once in a while, I'd kiss her on the cheek or forehead. This went on until about 5 pm, then she said I need help.

"Honey, do you want to go back to the hospital?" I whispered in her ear.

She said no, I need help from God. That just broke my heart, I started to cry and had a hard time keeping it from her.

A caretaker came in. I told her Erna was getting worse. "No," the caretaker said, "she just had a panic attack. I will give her some medication and she will be alright."

Well I took the caretaker at her word and told Erna I was going to leave. Erna said "thanks for sticking with me through this."

I told Erna not to worry I would have stayed with her for as long as it would take. Then, I left.

On Friday morning the phone rang around 7am. The caretaker said, "Mr Thomas, Erna is not doing well at all. How far away are you from here? I think you should try to get here as soon as you can."

I drove like a maniac to get there. When I walked in, a caretaker met me at the door and said Mr. Thomas I am sorry, but Erna has passed. It felt like someone stuck me in the heart. I bawled like a baby.

Erna passed away on April 28, 2011 at approximately 7:30 am.

& Life Goes On...

**ERNA
My Best Friend &
Love of my Life**

Chapter Twenty Two

My Life without Erna

My life right after Erna's passing was miserable. I was very sad, lonely, and depressed. But I had to keep going. I passed my time by working on my antique tractors, working at the Ivy Bend Volunteer Fire department on old worn out fire trucks. I was also a member of the Fire Board.

I worked to pass the time without my lifelong buddy.

Red Tractor

There would be an old tractor out in a field or at someone's shed, I'd feel sorry for it and buy it. I'd bring it home and tear it completely down, fix what needed to be repaired by straightening out sheet metal, painting it. I'd get it ready for parades either at Versailles, Cole Camp, Ivy Bend, or at the Owensville Threshers show in Rosebud, MO. I purchased an 18-foot tandem axle trailer to transport the tractors to towns for parades and shows.

In April of 2012 I talked to daughter Pam, who was deeply depressed with the upcoming anniversary of Erna's passing. I decided to take a train out to California to be with her during the anniversary.

It took two full days to travel from Sedalia, Missouri to California. The human hind-end is not made to sit for 48 hours. As soon as Pam picked me up at the rail terminal, I went to the ticket office and arranged to have a sleeper booth for the way home.

Pam and Ric made plans to celebrate my birthday on the 24th of April. Ric rented a small motorized 'scow' which had a clear plastic cover to keep tourists from getting wet in rain or from the sea spray of other boats. Pam made a pineapple upside down cake (my favorite) and brought it along. We celebrated my birthday with champagne.

When we'd been at Pam's in previous years, Erna had loved to walk out on the long pier at Seal Beach and watch the surfers, and the sea gulls and dolphins play. Pam bought some rose petals and on the April 28th, we walked out on the pier and scattered the petals into the Ocean. We both cried quite a bit then.

After we moved to the new lake home for full retirement, I went to the Columbia Missouri Veterans Administration (VA) for all my treatment beginning in 2005.

Sometime after Erna's passing, the VA told me I had a serious heart issue. I required special treatment and new medications. In 2013, with new medications, I was running around this earth with a 36, or 38 pulse. I was so weak I couldn't hardly do anything. All I wanted to do was sleep.

When I went to the VA Clinics at St. James, Jefferson City or Columbia, the nurses took my blood pressure. My pulse was 36, or 38 but the nurses didn't say anything so I just plugged along.

I made an appointment with a cardiac Doctor at the Columbia, VA and was fitted with a heart monitor to wear for three months. The monitor is about the size of a small shoe box and weighs around 10 lbs. I wore it all the time, except when showering. The six monitor attachments were stuck on my body.

Sometimes when I slept, one of the stick-on leads would come loose. The monitor made a squeaky sound to wake me up. Then I'd feel around and stick the lead back on. It was boring to wear the monitor, but I never learned of any issues with it.

My primary care nurse told me her father had been living with low pulse readings for years. I told her I am not your father. I'm not going to continue to be a couch potato for the rest of my life, I want something done.

During one of the low pulse days, I was working out in the garage when I passed out on the driveway, knocking a hole in my forehead. It required stitches. I went into the house and told my friend Marge I needed a band aid.

Marge looked at the wound and said, "Yeah you really need a band aid. I am going to take you over to the ambulance people and have them look at it."

As soon as we got there one of the paramedics started to clean the blood. Another paramedic took my blood pressure and was very concerned about my low pulse. He asked me how long have I had been living with this low pulse. I told him for most of a year.

I told the paramedics I just wanted to get the hole fixed so I could go home. Wrong. The paramedic said I should go to a hospital.

I disagreed and argued with him. Marge stepped in and said I should go to the hospital.

I finally gave in, and I told the paramedic he had to check with the VA and see if they had any beds. No beds were available so they took me to the nearest hospital, St. Mary's in Jefferson City. I was assigned a different cardiac heart specialist, Dr. Deliginol.

Dr. Deliginol was not a VA doctor. He worked for St. Mary's Hospital and was considered one of the best heart doctors in Missouri. So being his patient, I got the best possible care for my heart.

He asked me what meds the VA was giving me for my heart problems and I told him. Dr. Deliginol was shocked. He told me those meds were causing me to live with the low pulse. He immediately took those meds away and started me on new meds. During the days I was at the hospital my pulse started to coming up. I had appointments with Dr. Deliginol for over a year, until he retired.

Chapter Twenty Three

Picking up the Pieces

In August 2012, I received a letter about a high school class reunion at Owensville. For years Erna and I attended most of the high school reunions and she always enjoyed going. I just went because she wanted to go. So I didn't want to go without Erna by my side. I just wrote a letter with a picture of me sitting alongside my John Deere tractor. I told them about my life as a bachelor.

While visiting with Marge Oney (Brockman) and Verna at the reunion, Verna asked Marge if she'd read the letter I had sent in. Marge read the letter. I don't know what Marge was thinking when she read my letter. But Marge wrote a letter to me. She knew my brother Gerald lived in St. Charles, not too far from her place.

In her letter, Marge said if I ever came to St. Charles to visit my brother, I could give her a call and we could visit. Well I didn't answer her letter and a little later on in the year, I got a Halloween card from Marge. I was 77 years old and I'd never gotten a Halloween card from anyone. I said to myself, she is fishing.

But after the Halloween card I did give her a call. We talked for several hours. She invited me to come visit her sometime in St. Charles. So I did go and visit her, and I slept in a lower bedroom at her beautiful villa.

Marge had lost her husband in 2004 to cancer. She has no siblings and no children. She lost a baby during childbirth in her earlier years. She asked if she could come to my lake home and live there with me for a while. She was lonely there by herself having only a few friends in the general area where she lived. I agreed to have her come.

I picked Marge up at Verna's, near Drake, Missouri on a windy, snowy day. I drove back to the lake in a hell of a snow storm. The wind almost blew me off the highway a couple of times. But she was with me for Christmas.

My daughter Pam came to visit me shortly after Christmas. She stayed for several days. Both Pam and Marge kept talking to me about leaving the lake, maybe going back to Owensville. Well I thought about that idea for quite a while. It really wouldn't take much for me to move. I was so lonely at the lake without Erna.

In January 2013, Gloria, Erna's sister informed me that a little house in Owensville was on the market. I just loved the little house, Erna's great Uncle Will had built it in 1972. Uncle Will was a farmer and a carpenter by trade. The little house is made of brick, and has a beautiful, dry, basement. It is on a nice lot with a fence around it.

Uncle Will and Aunt Annie (brother and sister) lived there for quite some time. When they passed, they left the house to their niece Hilda Moeller.

The house was refurbished by the owners who bought if after Hilda's passing. They replaced the counter tops, in the kitchen, put tile in both bathrooms. They installed laminate floors in all the rooms and knocked out part of the wall dividing the front room and kitchen.

I couldn't get to Owensville fast enough to look at it and make a decision to purchase it. Agent Lavern Brandhorse made an appointment and took me to tour of the house. It is not really large, but it's comfortable for me and Marge.

I decided to sell my lake property and move back to Owensville. I started the process of selling and I had so much stuff to deal with before the move. I got in touch with an Amish auction business in Versailles. The auction people came to the lake with a huge trailer and barely got it all in the trailer. All of the helpers commented on the helpful notes I'd put on each box. There was a short description of what was in each box and where to take it in the Owensville house. I don't know how many trips I made from the basement to the garage, carrying stuff up for the auction.

Living at a lake with all kinds of trees, makes the leaves a tremendous chore to remove. The leaves were pretty thick around the lake house. I just decided not rake and burn them, just to let them lay. On one of my trips from the garage to the basement I slipped on some ice that was buried under the leaves and fell backwards, landing on my right side just below the right shoulder blade. It hurt forever. Unfortunately the pain comes back to this day when I overuse my back muscles.

To prepare the lake house for sale I got the septic tank inspected to make sure it wouldn't require any expensive repairs. I installed new carpeting in the living room and the master bedroom.

I came to the Owensville house a couple of times before the move. The master bedroom was a beige color. I painted the kid's room (my computer room now) eggshell white. I painted it one coat and thought it was enough, but several people voted against me so I gave in for the second coat but they helped me do it. Gloria and Gene worked hard in the house putting new shelf paper in cabinets and drawers. I really appreciated all of their help. I also brought four tier shelving to put in the basement for storage.

I set February 19th for the big move. The house was on the market but it wasn't sold at moving time. I told my daughter Cindy and her husband Jim that I was moving back to Owensville. I told my sister in law Mary Lou, and other friends and relatives about the move.

February 19th is Mary Lou's birthday so Pat Schmidt made a small cake and we had a little birthday party just before we started to load the U-Haul truck. The morning of the move,

Cindy, Jim, Joe a lake neighbor, Pat and Glenn Schmidt, Mary Lou, Mary Lou's son, Dale, Roger Biles, Mary Lou's brother, and Marge all helped to get the furniture, pictures, utensils clothing and everything else into the vehicles. Mary Lou loaded her pickup with all sorts of stuff. She even had the passenger side of her truck seat loaded down. We were ready to be on our way by 10:30am.

When we all started to get in our vehicles. Marge asked me, "Major, who am I going to ride with?" I said Mary Lou. So Mary Lou had to take all the stuff she'd put in her pickup elsewhere. I don't know where she fit it all in, but somehow, she did.

We arrived in Owensville around 1pm and started the unloading. I mainly directed traffic and tried to keep a little order. Cindy was in charge of the pictures! Gene carried stuff down to the basement here comes Cindy back up the stairs, Gene asked her what are you doing here I am carrying stuff down stairs and here are you carrying stuff back up? Cindy told Gene I am getting all the pictures hung all over the house, she even put pictures on the walls in the basement. Most of the pictures she hung that day are still in place. Roger took charge getting the washer and dryer hooked up.

All the unloading was finished by 3pm. We got the U haul truck back right away. Mary Lou made a nice stew for us to snack on. So that day was over with by evening time. The weather was great, pleasantly warm, no wind to speak of, and the sun was out all day.

I was born in a Catholic hospital and Orphanage. It was 1934. I was adopted, the adoption was finalized in 1936. My adoptive Mother was a very dedicated Catholic and she made my adoptive father promise to allow me to join the Catholic Church and go to the Catholic school. My adoptive father agreed to let my mother guide me through the 9 years I spent at Little Flower Catholic School. I was an altar boy throughout those years.

Even after we moved to Owensville in 1948, I served as an altar boy. I served as altar boy during the corner stone laying ceremony after the new church was built in 1949. And eventually, we got married. But Erna and I got married out of the Catholic Church. I was never proud of myself for doing that.

After Erna's passing when I moved back to Owensville I wanted to get back into the Catholic Church. I went to the Catholic Church and met Father Francis. He is a very understanding person and he vowed to help me. He knew a priest in Neier, Missouri who was starting a session for people wanting to get back to the Catholic Church. The classes were every Tuesday evening at 7 pm.

I cannot drive at night, so Mary Lou, my beloved sister in law drove me and she attended the sessions. We learned a lot about the church. The sessions lasted until Easter. At the Easter service, Father Kevin introduced all of the class members to the congregation and handed us each of a small-type bible. So I am a member of the Catholic Church and I attend mass every Saturday evening.

I have made some improvements while living in my house over the years. I installed a new roof, a new driveway and glass shower doors in main bath room. I had a 10' by 20' shed built for storing tractors, the riding mower, my golf cart and other implements. I sold the little shed in southwest corner of the yard and put a privacy fence alongside the north side of the patio. I had an 18' sliding gate installed on north fence in front of the new shed, and put a new water softener in basement. ..

Chapter Twenty Four

The Honor Flight

I was invited to attend meetings at the local VFW. At the VFW, I was coaxed into filing an application for an Honor Flight. But during this time I came down with my heart issues.

I had an appointment at the VA to see my cardiac doctor. She wanted to put me on new meds for the heart problems. She took my (very effective) sleep meds away because the new heart meds would conflict with my present sleep meds. I told them in so many words they'd better give me a sleep med that would be effective. But they gave me some sleep meds that didn't work, period.

So I worked with the VA as they tried to get me effective sleep meds. I went for one session that lasted for 6 nights with no sleep and another session for 9 nights without sleep. What a horrible time in my life. I told them to help me or I might do something to myself. Then I got a behavior health nurse who found me a combination of meds that worked and is still working.

Dr. Deliginol at St. Mary's Hospital told me that I should get a pacemaker, but he was reluctant to make the effort for me to get one. He wasn't sure what type of pacemaker I should have, a two or three wire.

Dr. Deliginol asked me if I would see a specialist. I agreed, if it would get me closer to getting a pacemaker. He set up an appointment with a Dr. Pierce at University Hospital in Columbia. After a test or two, Dr. Pierce said I should have had a pacemaker a long time ago. Within a few weeks, the three wire pacemaker was installed in October 2013.

The Honor Flight system was developed by several veterans. The basic plan is to transport veterans from any and all wars to Washington, D.C. to visit their respective memorials.

The organizers got with Southwest airlines and Southwest volunteered to pay for the veterans air fare to Washington. Other participants and organizers had to pay their own way. My beloved brother in law went as my guardian and he had to pay his own way.

There is another Honor Flight organization in Columbia Missouri. The Honor Flight we attended was called the Franklin County Honor Flight.

In mid-summer 2013, I received a notice from the Franklin County Honor Flight that explained what I had to do to prepare for the trip. My brother in law Gene, volunteered to be my guardian. All vets on Honor Flights must have a Guardian. The Guardians must pay their own way for the flight. Vets paid nothing.

The flight date was October 2, 2013. That was the second day of the big government shutdown. No fountains were working at any of the memorials and no rest-rooms were open. If we had to use a rest room, we used the one on the coach.

We were privileged to have a Vietnam veteran who got special permission to go on our tour to see his Vietnam memorial. He was terminally ill. During the time I went on the Honor Flight, the tours were mostly for Korea War veterans, and a few WWII vets.

& Life Goes On...

We were fortunate to have a professional tour guide who described landmarks and other prominent locations in Washington to us. The tour guide told us the Pentagon was built in just eighteen months. He also said that it was so hastily built that workers are to this day still correcting things the original builders forgot or did not do correctly.

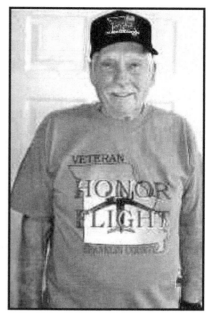

Gene, my beloved Guardian picked me up around 1am in the morning on October 2nd. We went to Washington, Missouri and boarded a large coach that transported us to the St. Louis airport. When we arrived at the airport, our special Vietnam vet played taps for us. It was a privilege to listen to the taps he played.

He played taps at every war memorial we visited. Several times it brought tears to our eyes, especially at Arlington Cemetery and the tomb of the Unknown Soldier. There wasn't a dry eye anywhere. We visited the Vietnam memorial, the Vietnam wall, the World War II memorial, the Korea War memorial and the Air Force Memorial.

Unfortunately, there are some very disrespectful people who visit some of the memorials. They show no emotion and little respect for the memorials: especially at the tomb of the Unknown Soldier. Sometimes, the guards have to yell at these unpatriotic individuals and tell them to keep quiet. We dealt with that type of situation when we visited.

When we arrived at Memorial Plaza there were dozens of people there, along with several TV stations. I was at the gates in a wheel chair where Gene had positioned me. The cameras were rolling. There was a lot of commotion when the gates opened.

As we entered the plaza, Gene's son texted him and told him we were on TV.

The Tomb Guard Sentinels guard the Tomb of the Unknown Soldier with military precision and impeccable honor. The guard changes every hour on the hour. An impeccably uniformed commander appears at the Plaza to announce the changing of the guard.

Soon, the new sentinel leaves the quarters, unlocking the bolt of his or her M14 rifle. This signals the relief commander and the current commander at the center of the path in front of the tomb. All three salute the Unknown, who has been symbolically given the Medal of Honor.

The relief commander orders the relieved sentinel, "a pass on your orders".

The current sentinel replies "pass on your orders".

The current commander commands, "Post orders remains as directed".

The newly-posted sentinel replies "orders acknowledged". Then steps into position on the black mat in front of the tomb.

When the relief commander passes by, the new sentinel begins walking at a cadence of 90 steps per minute. The tomb guard marches 21 steps down the black mat behind the tomb, turns, faces east for 21 seconds, turns, faces north, for 21 seconds, then takes 21 steps down the mat, and repeats the process. The 21 seconds chosen symbolizes the highest military honor that can be bestowed: the 21 gun salute....

Guards commit to two years of guarding the tomb. They must live in a barracks under the tomb and cannot drink any alcohol on or off duty for rest of their lives. They cannot swear in public for rest of their lives.

After two years each guard is given a wreath pin. The guards must live by the rules they swore to, for the rest of their lives.

During the first six months of duty a guard cannot talk to anyone or watch TV. All off-duty time is to be spent studying the 175 people laid to rest, and learning where they are interred. They must remember this for the rest of their lives.

The Korea War Memorial, was the most moving for me because of serving three tours of duty in Korea. The person who designed the Memorial wanted to have 38 soldiers in the field with their ponchos on, but he was only allowed half. So he went a bit further. He built a reflective wall and the reflection of the soldiers in the field shows 38 soldiers.

The number 38 refers to the 38th parallel which divides South and North Koreas.

From St. Louis, we arrived at the Baltimore Airport but on departure we left from Reagan National Airport. We were fed at the airport before leaving Baltimore.

A pleasant surprise awaited us on the plane. The Franklin County Honor Flight organizers made arrangements with each veteran's family and friends, to write letters offering congratulations, words of love and affection. So a big bag of mail was distributed to each vet. I got 58 letters. Some letters were from people I didn't know and there were some from local school children. After reading a few of the letters filled with so much love and praise, it caused a few tears to flow.

We left Reagan National Airport late in the evening, heading back to St. Louis. Upon our arrival, my brother in law and sister in law: Glenn and Pat Schmidt were there to greet me. What a surprise!

There were dozens and dozens of motorcycle vets there to greet us. They awaited our departure and escorted us back to Washington, Missouri. We were presented with pictures taken that day. And there were awards for some.

Major Thomas

The coach drivers and the Missouri Highway Patrolmen donated their time to transport us, we had the motor cycle 'patriots' and Highway Patrol escorts.

With all the pleasant surprises, getting to see our memorials, the pleasant flight back and forth and all the complimentary comments from the flight crew, nothing else could have been more rewarding. I finally got to my home in Owensville around midnight, making it a 23 hour day. It is an event that will be on my mind until the day I die.

& Life Goes On...

Chapter Twenty Five

Life in Owensville These Days

Marge became seriously ill with pneumonia. I called the local ambulance service to transport her to Mercy Hospital in Washington, Missouri. She stayed in the hospital for five days before I could bring her home. Several days later she became ill again, so I took her back to the hospital where she remained for seven more days with the same symptoms. The hospital had released her too early and she still had the pneumonia bug.

Years ago when we were living at the Lake, Erna kept asking, "Why don't you get us a golf cart?" I finally gave in. We shopped around and located one in Versailles. We purchased one. I wanted Erna to drive it, for when she wanted to go over to daughter Cindy's. She never did it. I sold it when I left the Lake so I wouldn't have to transport it to Owensville.

Then I got the bug to get a golf cart in Owensville. I located one at A & J sales in St. Clair, Missouri. It's a Yamaha with a nice Harley Davidson paint job. We bought it in May 2015. Marge and I enjoy driving it around Owensville. At first, the Owensville police didn't bother us when we were running around town.

Now, golf cart owners must pass a City inspection by the Police department. We have to have proof of insurance, proof of ownership and a safety panel installed.

For my 80th birthday, Gene and Gloria took me and Mary Lou to Cuba, Missouri to the Country Kitchen for a brunch. If I remember right it was my eightieth. Gloria had a hat, something like a helmet with a big yellow 80 on the front and some banners. It was a fun day.

For the 2014 Thresher's show, I transported three vehicles to Rosebud. I took the 1949 Ford 8N tractor, the 1944 Model B John Deere tractor and the Conestoga wagon. Every year, the event is in the middle of July so the temperature is usually in the upper '90's. So I needed help driving one of the tractors. I don't remember who helped me that year, but I appreciate it.

My daughter Pam requested that we come visit her in California in 2014. The visit with Pam was good for all of us. We had a good time together. It was the sunshine before the storm.

& Life Goes On...

Marge has a second cousin, Terry. She and her husband Jeff live in Baton Rouge, Louisiana. Terry's husband Jeff owns a timeshare at Massanutten, Virginia in the Shenandoah River Valley. Massanutten is an Indian tribe's name.

Marge and I were invited to spend Memorial Day weekend 2015 at their family reunion in Virginia. So we flew from St. Louis to Baltimore, Maryland to meet Terry and Jeff. They picked us up for the trip to their Massanutten time share.

We met many other family members including: Scott and his wife Julie (second cousin to Marge), Rod who is Julie's brother and Madison, a third cousin to Marge.

We had a great time there. There was time to just rest, visit and go for walks together. We went to Massanutten Mountain and walked to the top. The view was impressive. We visited a horse ranch where we petted the horses and watched their antics as they played in the corrals. We enjoyed fabulous meals, watched TV and had fun.

Marge and I had a private bedroom with twin beds. During the night when I got up, I got tangled up in a huge comforter laying partially on the floor. I fell backwards, landing on my neck and shoulders. I saw stars, little birdies and felt a tingling up and down my back.

I really didn't think I was hurt, but I had a little dizziness the following day. As soon as we arrived back in Owensville, I called the VA.

When I told them about my fall, the VA insisted I get a CAT scan as soon as possible. It was a couple of weeks before I got the CAT scan. The doctor said the scan showed nothing out of order, but I might have problems in the future.

In 2015, I needed a more reliable riding lawn mower, so I purchased a new 42" John Deere. Boy, it makes my yard work easier

I also got the bug to get a new pickup. I shopped around on the internet and finally located the one I wanted at Auffenberg Ford in Washington, Missouri. It's a pretty blue. Marge and I took possession on March 31, 2015. I got some extras for it: a customized grill, a chrome grill guard, a roll back bed cover, chrome fender trim and chrome window covers.

On the morning of August 11, 2015, I couldn't stand up straight. I walked bent over with my arms extended toward the floor so as not to fall on my face. I already had an appointment that day with the VA but I called the VA hospital to tell them I could not drive and called an ambulance to transport me to the hospital.

It is protocol to call the VA to see if they have beds available. There were no beds available so the VA told the paramedics to transport me to St. Mary's Hospital in Jefferson City, Missouri. I arrived at the hospital around 9am. I went into the Emergency Room for evaluation: they did blood tests, took EKG tests and other stuff. After the frenzy all got quiet, everyone left and no one else came back in the room until 3pm. I laid there all that time with no other visits from hospital staff.

Finally, the doctor came in the room and pulled up a chair close to my bed. He said they couldn't find anything that could have brought on my symptoms. I looked at the doctor and said you might take a CAT scan and he asked me why.

I told the doctor that I had fallen over Memorial Day weekend and that I'd fallen backwards onto my neck. So he had the CAT scan performed. He came back in the room with his arms up in the air.

"You have a subdural hematoma, in simple laymen's terms, blood on the brain. It's not uncommon for a person who has suffered a fall like you have." He said. "I have an ambulance coming and it should be here in fifteen minutes to transport you to Columbia, Missouri, University Hospital for immediate surgery."

As soon as I arrived at the University Hospital, the procedure began. They shaved some hair off the top of my head, drilled two holes in my scalp and installed some sort of vacuum tubes to suck out the fluid.

The next morning, several doctors and nurses came in. Right off the bat, they asked me if I knew what day it was, if I knew where I was and if I knew what procedure I had the evening before. I answered all questions correctly. I told them I wanted to go home and they said they would take me on a walk around the hospital. If I didn't have any problems with balance, they would let me go home.

I was 81 years of age when this all went down. It was the first time that doctor ever saw me. I would think that a doctor with a new patient would ask questions about what the patient's activities were before coming to a hospital. Like, have you had any falls recently? Or, have you passed out or do you have other issues I might need to know about? But he didn't do that, so I told him about my health problems.

I had cataract surgery on October 20, 2015. It was not eventful. They did the surgery pretty early in the morning and I had to stick around the hospital until around 3pm. The surgeon inspected the surgery area and was satisfied, so I went home. It certainly improved my eyesight.

After the episode of the blood on my brain surgery, and after the wonderful care the paramedics gave me to get me to the hospital, I just couldn't say enough about the professional care they gave me.

I met Nick then, he's a paramedic. Karen, the Owensville Ambulance head person was asking around trying to find a new board member to fill an empty slot. Nick recommended me for the job. Karen came to my home and interviewed me about my background and asked some other pertinent questions to see if I qualified.

I have been an Ambulance board member for about three years. We have meetings that last from 6 to 10pm about every other month. I really enjoy time spent with the wonderful people there at the station.

In the spring of 2016, we were invited to Terry and Jeff's in Baton Rouge. We flew into the New Orleans airport. Terry picked us up there and drove us to their home in Baton Rouge. That was on a Thursday. Jeff had to work on that Friday so Terry took us on a tour of downtown Baton Rouge, the state capital.

The Louisiana state capital is impressive. It is the tallest state capital building in the nation: it is 450 feet high with 34 stories. It was built in 14 months. A tour guide at the capital was just getting off duty, but he took us on a private tour. He told us they had to drive in piers seven miles deep to support the massive building, I don't believe it to this day. The capital grounds are adorned with beautiful flowers.

At the top there is an observation deck which allows for a grand view of the surrounding area and downtown. There was a personal elevator for Huey P. Long, governor of the State from 1928 to 1932. Huey was assassinated while at the capital preparing for a session with state legislators.

During our visit, Terry took me to the ship museum tied up in the downtown area for a tour of the U.S.S. Kidd, a World War II Fletcher class destroyer. Erna and I had toured the Kidd years before and I really enjoyed it. The U.S.S. Kidd D.D. 661 was launched February 1943 at the Federal Shipbuilding and Dry Dock Company.

The Kidd was assigned to the Pacific Theater to provide fire power for invasions at Leyte Gulf, and other Pacific islands. She was struck during the Okinawa Invasion by a kamikaze plane on the starboard side, killing 38 crew members and wounding 55 others.

I toured her for the second time, inside and out, and I enjoyed the entire tour. I talked with several volunteers, three of whom served aboard LST's during WWII. I asked them how many volunteers they had aboard, they said five. When they were getting the Kidd secured at the present mooring on the Mississippi River, then starting the rebuilding, they had 200 volunteers,

Terry then took us to the University of Louisiana campus. What a striking and huge campus that was!

For the weekend, Terry and Jeff packed up essentials for taking to 'Camp'. At lakes, rivers and other sites in the northern states, we call our campsites, 'Camps'. Anyway Terry and Jeff's 'camp' was a very nice cabin that was around 12 feet off the ground to deal with constant floods.

Saturday, Jeff and I went over to a dock that a relative of Terry's used. We removed a lot of rotted deck timbers and planks. We worked pretty hard that day.

But we had a wonderful time and were treated with the utmost care while we visited. We returned to St. Louis on Monday.

The VA made me an appointment with a Dr. Golda on February 9, 2016 to remove cancer cells from my left ear. That was an all-day project. What a procedure!

Daughter Pam and Ric came to Owensville at Thanksgiving time. They stayed at the local motel for the three days they were here. They took the train from Los Angeles, it took them two days to get to St. Louis. Then they drove out in the afternoon from St. Louis. They didn't get here until late in the evening so they didn't come to the house until the next day.

Pam came over around 9am and started visiting. Ric stayed at the motel and slept in because he'd worked late on his computer. Around 1:30pm, Ric called Pam to bring him to the house. He wanted Pam to cook him breakfast. I'd asked Pam before they came, what kind of food we needed to get for them. Pam said Ric always had Canadian bacon and eggs for his breakfast. Pam said she wanted plenty of Dr. Pepper soda on hand. She drank Dr. Pepper all day long, I don't know how many bottles she drank.

Well, Ric worked on his computer at our house, he didn't visit with any of us. Then about 3pm, he asked Pam to take him back to the hotel because he had much more to do on his computer.

Rick had packed a suitcase for each day he would be gone from home. When they got to St. Louis, he'd gotten his computer out to work with it while waiting at the train station, but it didn't work. So, he spent two days here trying to get the computer to work. The next day he worked late into the night and slept in. Pam came to our house around 9am. Pam brought him to the house around 1pm. Repeat.

The computer still wasn't working so he asked me if I knew anybody at Walmart who might help him to get the computer working. Well, I do have a wonderful friend who works in the Electronics Department, so I took Ric over to Walmart. I caught Cody walking towards the breakroom, he was going on break and I hollered at him. I introduced them. Ric told Cody about his computer so Cody offered to help. Cody gave up his break time to help Ric. They worked on it for about an hour: nothing.

Cody called the computer company and talked to a technician there. After another hour, he finally got it working. Then Ric just started to walk off. I said to wait a minute, he needed to at least thank Cody for using up two hours of his time to get the computer working. I walked back to Cody and sincerely thanked him for what he had done.

Then Ric wanted to have supper. He suggested we get a couple of pizzas for dinner so we stopped by Dominos and brought pizza home. We settled down at the dinner table. All he talked about was himself. Around 5:30pm, he told Pam he wanted to get back to the motel, he had work to do. That was the last I saw of him. He probably spent 5 hours with us while in Owensville, glad to get rid of him.

The VA made an appointment with a dermatologist at the University Boone County Hospital to have a large area of cancer cells below my left ear surgically removed. The surgery lasted all day and required 28 stitches. It took a long time to heal.

The Schmidt family and my family have a beloved Aunt Lydia who is still living her life happily in a care center in Owensville, Missouri.

Aunt Lydia celebrated her 101st birthday in January, 2019. You go Aunt Lydia!

Chapter Twenty Six

My Daughter Pam

My daughter Pam and her husband Ric went to Dallas to spend Christmas with his family. While they were in Dallas, Pam became very ill. She was placed in ICU and in a coma for two days.

Ric said he was germephobic so he couldn't go to Pam's room to check on her. He didn't want to go near a hospital. One of Ric's family members told him he needed to go see Pam, it wasn't right to not see his wife. But he never went to see her while she was in the hospital.

Our family didn't know Pam was in the hospital until the word got out. Pam had a close friend who worked with her in Seal Beach. She told my daughter Cindy and our family what Pam had reported about how Ric was treating her. That's when we first heard about Pam's hospital stay got out. So their marriage wasn't very good as far as we could tell. And Pam was miserable.

Pam lived a very stressful life. Pam had serious health issues which she inherited from her mother. Her job was very demanding, she often worked 12 to 15 hours a day. She was constantly driving in the terrible Los Angeles traffic. She often had to be a couple of hundred miles from home very early in the morning, then would work until late at night.

& Life Goes On...

She worked for a German company that makes hospital equipment. Sometimes the company manufactured inferior equipment that Pam would unknowingly sell to hospitals. The nurses and doctors could get very upset about the inferior product. Pam, being the 'front-man' often took the brunt of their anger. Sometimes their language was vulgar and very insulting. But Pam lived with it. I am sure it hurt her to the core.

Her husband worked for himself and on his own schedule. He was at home all day while she was out. He called her his trophy wife. After working long hard hours all week, Pam would get home and want to relax. But Ric would be ready to go out. He laid out her clothes and insisted that she come with him to meet his cronies at high-end bars and restaurants. Pam was just exhausted, but she never felt like she had a choice.

Ric told all of us that he was a helicopter pilot, that he had driven 18 wheelers, worked on ranches, and in the oil fields. His stories went on and on.

He told his friends he was working for the CIA, doing clandestine operations. Pam would get so upset about his stories that she'd get up and go to the rest room to hide out for a while.

One evening she asked Ric about getting cleaning lady to help her around the house. Ric said no. After that, Pam decided to get away from him. She packed her suitcase and went to a hotel for several days, never telling Ric where she was. That had been a long time coming. We believed Ric kept egging her on and not giving her any help or compassion.

Pam called me and would say, "Dad, guess where I am?"

"I know where you are, stuck on a LA freeway traffic." I'd say to her. Those times when she called me is when we had our most beneficial phone talks.

"Yeah, I've got 20 miles to go and it will take me another two hours to get there." Pam would say. During some of those conversations she was so despondent. "Dad, I don't want to be here anymore," she would say.

Many times when Ric and Pam visited with us before Erna died, or visited Marge and me later, she'd tell a story. Ric would stop her in the middle to correct her. That was very embarrassing to Pam. It hurt her feelings to be belittled in front of her friends and family.

My beautiful daughter Pam, committed suicide on April 7, 2017. Even with all of the problems Pam had, it still was a terrible shock to our family.

Daughter Pam with her beloved Dog

I talked to Ric once after Pam's passing. He was worried about losing Pam's company health insurance and income. Pam was the primary bread winner.

My daughters were very close, they corresponded almost every day. Cindy talked to Pam on Thursday evening the sixth of April. When Cindy tried to call Pam the next day she couldn't get Pam to respond. Cindy tried again on Saturday morning: no response. Cindy was upset, so she called Ric.

Pam had been missing. Ric had called the local law enforcement to report her missing. So Ric didn't know anything about Pam's whereabouts on Saturday morning.

"Why are you calling now?" He asked Cindy, because he still didn't have any news. Ric knew Cindy didn't know about Pam's disappearance. Cindy told Ric she'd been trying to call Pam, but had no luck. Ric told Cindy Pam was missing. Early Monday morning, the Los Angeles County Coroner's Office called to inform Ric they found Pam.

Now thinking about Cindy, who kept calling Ric on Sunday and Monday. Ric told Cindy that Pam had been found and she was dead. That was April 10th.

What we know about Pam's death is limited. Pam had a dog, she'd always had one. She so loved animals. Often, she took her dog Savanah to a little park where dogs could play and be walked.

Friday evening, she went to the little park, without Savanah. There, she took I don't know how many Benadryl type medications. That is how she took her life.

Pam had recently had an accident with the company car, so she was driving a very small insurance company vehicle. She always had boxes of company equipment in her larger car. One of Pam's bosses had come the week before her death and she was embarrassed about having the small car. It was another stressful issue for her.

The conservation park officer saw the little car parked by the guard rail on the parking lot, but he didn't think much about it. He'd seen cars parked there with stuff in the back seat before that belonged to homeless people. When he saw Pam's junky car with the whole back end loaded with boxes, he thought nothing of it. A police patrol car officer found her car and reported it.

After Cindy called Ric on Monday and Ric told her about Pam, she knew she had to tell me. Cindy didn't want me to hear it on the phone so she called Mary Lou to get Reverend Van Lahmeyer to meet her at my house.

Cindy and Jim drove from the lake to my home. I thought that was very considerate of Cindy and Jim to do that. Marge and I were out on the patio visiting with my friend Zane and his mother. I couldn't believe it when Cindy, Jim, Mary Lou and Reverend Van Lahmeyer drove up. Then Cindy told me about Pam. It just broke my heart.

During the time of making preparations for Pam's celebration of life service Marge was a big help. She went to St. Charles to get her taxes done before April 15th but she quickly returned. The whole family was busy with the preparations.

Cindy worked hard preparing the obituary for Pam, and it was very wonderful. I put it in the Owensville paper for three weeks.

Reverend Van officiated the celebration of life service at the St. Paul Cooper Hill church. The church women prepared a wonderful reception meal. We had an organist and a couple of friends sang a few hymns. I put the notice of Pam's service in the Owensville paper. Memorial Day was the day of the service.

The day was a bad one: very stormy, rainy and windy. The storm blew down trees across the roadways. But the turnout was heartwarming.

& *Life Goes On...*

The church was full of friends and relatives. Cindy made a beautiful picture board. People came from the Lake and old neighbors came from Kansas City. It was a rewarding day.

Chapter Twenty Seven

Health and Happiness

My birthday came around again in 2017. Gene and Gloria took Marge and I, to Jefferson City to a very unique museum just east of the city. I spent most of the afternoon enjoying all the exhibits: all military. Then they took us to Prison Brews, a restaurant in Jefferson City.

In mid-summer 2017, I know God was watching over me and gave me a clue that I needed to rid myself of my two antique tractors. I was getting weaker as time went by. I wanted to transport my tractors to the Owensville Threshers show in Rosebud, but I just couldn't stand the excessive heat.

I was having a difficult time pulling out and lifting the heavy ramps to the back of the trailer, that's why God wanted me to get rid of the tractors. To make the final decision was very difficult.

I decided to give my son in law Jim, the 44 John Deere. I called Jim and asked him if he wanted it. Of course he was delighted! Jim and Cindy came up a week later to pick it up.

Then I asked Gene Ridder if he would want the 1958 International. He said yes. I waited to see for sure if he wanted it.

& Life Goes On...

1944 John Deere Model 'B'

Well, he couldn't stay away. He came over to the house and asked if I was going to give him the tractor. I said yes, I will bring it down to the farm. He stuck around for a few minutes, like he was waiting for me to hook my pickup up and load the tractor on it. So he helped me get it loaded and unloaded at the farm. Just a few weeks later, on the last day of September I had a serious and near-fatal heart attack.

1958 International 230

On the morning of September 30, 2017, I was talking to Marge and glancing at the TV, when I started to feel nauseous. I broke into a sweat, and felt like I had a Sherman Tank laying on the right side of my chest. I even had trouble with my sight.

Since I'd never had a heart attack before, I had to make a decision about whether to call an ambulance or not. Marge immediately made me take an 81 MG baby aspirin which I know it helped a lot before the ambulance arrived. The paramedics knew I was having a heart attack, and they started treating me because of my symptoms right away.

On the way to the hospital I thought it would never end. The ambulance driver took a route towards Jefferson City. Highway 89 is one of the most crooked roads in the area. I was disorientated and my stomach was upset, the paramedics gave some kind of medication to help with the upset stomach.

The driver called the VA to see if they had a bed available and of course, there was no bed. The driver was told to take me to St. Mary's Hospital. We arrived at the Emergency Room where they took all my vital signs and started taking care of me.

I was in ICU for most of the day and was monitored very closely the whole time. Then I was taken to a room upstairs where I stayed until my release. Early the following morning, Dr. Sanfelippo. He ordered an ECHO procedure immediately even though it was Sunday morning.

He said he needed to find out what damage was done to the heart from the heart attack. Throughout my time in the hospital, they performed all kinds of X-rays, additional tests and blood draws.

For several days, Dr. Sanfelippo told me I had quite a bit of damage. If I had not had the pacemaker, I wouldn't have survived the heart attack. I was prescribed five more medications for care of the heart.

& Life Goes On...

The VA was after me with phone calls setting me up for 36 sessions of Cardiac Rehab. The closest hospital for rehab was Missouri Baptist in Sullivan, Missouri, which is 37 miles from Owensville. So I made 36 trips to Sullivan. There were two very nice, professional nurses who watched me closely, I wore a heart monitor during each session. At my last session, one of the nurses gave me a diploma that says on it: Certificate of Progress.

Before I had my heart attack Marge and I worked out at the local gym. After the completion of the rehab and the VA signed off, I could go back to doing my workouts at the local gym again. Now, I go three days a week and do three different machines for 20 minutes each. I went from 191 pounds down to 182 pounds, and holding.

Now, I have 16 doctor's appointments, dental, audiologist, heart specialists and lab work several times a year. My primary doctor in St. James. I see behavioral nurse. It just never ends.

My beautiful daughter, Pam's birthday was on the 26th of March. My friends and family: Gloria, Cindy, Pat, Mary Lou and Danna, all bumped heads. They called to see if Marge and I could make it to Jefferson City on that day to celebrate Pam's passing on her birthday instead of celebrating her passing on the day she did pass (April 7th). It all worked out well, so we met.

Mary Lou had a doctor's appointment that morning so she had to be in Jefferson City. I had a dentist appointment at 1:00pm for a root canal. We all met at 11:15 that morning to spend time together until I left around 12:30. PM. We had a nice visit and talked a lot about Pam.

I've been a board member of the Owensville Ambulance District for several years. I'm proud to serve such a wonderful organization. On April 18th the ambulance engineer called to meet with the Building Committee members to discuss the parking lot. There are four of us on that committee. I arrived right at noon.

Karen the administer saw me walking toward the entrance. I stepped in but right away Karen said step back outside for a moment. She asked me how I felt, I told her I felt okay. Karen said I looked very pale and was wobbly walking toward the door.

Within a few minutes she had three paramedics putting stick-ums all over my body to do an EKG, then came blood pressure tests and a lot of other stuff. The paramedic said I should go to a hospital. I said no.

The ambulance took me and insisted that I call the VA. Then she talked to the doctor or nurse and told them what they had noticed with all the tests they took at the ambulance site. The VA talked to me again and insisted I go to the hospital immediately.

So I really didn't have a choice. On the way, I told the paramedic he had to call the VA and see if they had a bed. The VA doctor asked the paramedic how far out they were. The paramedic said about an hour and half. Then the VA doctor told the paramedic to take me to a closer hospital, which was St. Mary's in Jefferson City.

The paramedic put me on an IV and by the time we got to the hospital I was about to pee in my pants. I got settled in at the Emergency Room and they put me on another IV bag. The hospital did all kinds of tests and concluded I was dehydrated. They were going to turn me loose, so I called my brother in law Gene Ridder asked him if he would come to Jefferson City to pick me up, which he did.

God had told me to get rid of my antique tractors, because of my health issues. Lifting out those heavy ramps from the rear of the trailer was just getting to me especially during the heat of the summer months.

Sometime in mid-August 2018, my niece Paige and kids stopped to visit with me for about an hour or so. Enjoyed the visit. Paige is the daughter of my sister in law and brother in law, Gene and Gloria Ridder

The middle of August 2018, my family's farm home on Old Springfield Road, just south of Owensville, where we moved to from St. Louis, burned to the ground. It was in dire neglect for around 20 years: it was all full of weeds. Trees, sprouts and saplings had taken over the entire property. It just made me sick to see it in such disrepair. But it hadn't been lived in for 20 years. It used to be a beautiful and well maintained property. My whole family was very proud of it.

Old Farm Home in Owensvlle

On September 4, 2018, a navy shipmate, Jim, called me late in the evening. He asked if he could come by the next day. Of course, I was excited to see him!

We'd stayed in touch over the years, mainly at ship reunions. Jim and his wife Peggy arrived around noon and we visited until around 4pm, then decided to go out to eat. We went to the Dinner Belle restaurant in Belle, Missouri. The food was great and we visited until around 5pm. Peggy seemed to enjoy the visit as well.

Jim wanted to be in Topeka, Kansas before dark. I told him there was no way, you will be lucky to be in Kansas City by dark.

A few years back, I was enjoying my breakfast at our favorite restaurant in Owensville. Marge wasn't with me. I noticed two women seating themselves at a table next to mine. I figured they were mother-daughter. The younger woman was wearing a headscarf like many women wear who are fighting cancer and in chemo. I understood just what she was feeling, because we lived through fighting Erna's cancer and the chemo. This young woman had to be feeling ill, threatened, and frightened.

After my meal, I sat beside her and asked if she was fighting cancer. She said yes. I felt so sorry for her. I thought it would be nice to help lift her spirits so, I hurried home, picked out a stained glass angel I had made and put a little white tissue around it. I put it in a small basket and hurried back to the restaurant to catch her before she left.

I gave her the angel. She unwrapped it and I saw a faint smile on her face and tear in her eye. It might have made her day

Just a few days ago, around the end of April, I had a chance meeting with her. I told her I was so happy to see that she survived the cancer and chemo. That made my day.

& Life Goes On...

Chapter Twenty Eight

Final Thoughts

I had a very sad start to the beginning of 2018, my beloved brother Gerald who was two years younger than me passed away on February 1, 2018. What a loss... A friend and brother through the many years of my life. I miss him so much.

My buddy for over six years now is Marge. For over sixty-five years, she's been fighting diabetes. She had a very dangerous event on November 30, 2018. Marge just passed out. She slipped off the living room couch and somehow, broke her ankle. She's been wearing a boot on her right foot ever since. She finally had to have surgery on her right ankle on March 1, 2019.

Marge still isn't out of the woods, she continues to be in need of greater care. As of this writing, she is Frene Valley Care Center in Owensville, Missouri. She is fighting a respiratory infection and they had to quarantine her for a week. Of course, she is ready to come home and we hope she gets discharged soon.

Several times, she's had to go to Mercy Hospital in Washington, Missouri via ambulance. One trip she was in horrific pain with both feet having neuropathy caused by the diabetes and her blood sugar levels. So, she's been out of circulation for about two months.

I have been so involved with my book and now, soon it will be published. I have so much support from my closer friends and relatives. Without their encouragement, I don't know how I could've gotten it done. My publisher has become my friend. She has the patience to help me get it done.

Major Thomas

I look back from my younger years to the present times. I am blessed to have old time friends who've stuck with me through all my health issues and Erna's health issues. They have been there when I was in good spirits and in times of depression.

In my later years, I've received support from some of my dearest relatives like my sisters-in-law: Mary Lou Thomas, Gloria Ridder and Pat Schmidt. I've had help from my brothers-in-law: Glenn Schmidt and Gene Ridder. My sister Marilyn Shoemaker, who has advised me and encouraged me throughout the process of getting my book printed. I also want to thank Matt Lenauer, a dear friend, who took his precious time to help me proof read both proofs. My dear friends: Tabitha Hurst, Anna Deimeke, and my neighbors Christen Knehans and her sons Zane and Jason, have all been there for me when I've needed them.

A couple of years ago, I had the privilege of meeting a very bright, energetic and mechanically-inclined young man. He and I have spent a lot of quality time together. I love him like I would love a son. He calls me Grandpa. I'm so proud of him because he is in welding college in Tulsa, Oklahoma. He will be graduating in the very near future – with top honors!

I had the privilege of meeting such a dear family friend: Pastor Van Lahmeyer, and his wife Juliette and son Mike. They have helped me through the painful loss of my youngest daughter Pamela. Pastor's prayers have helped me tremendously.

Overall, I've had a wonderful life filled with the love of my wife, friends and family. I believe if you live with your challenges and enjoy those people you love, if you pray to God and ask Him for help and guidance along the way, it will help you meet each day and hold onto this valuable thing called life.

It's why I'm here today, and my life goes on...

Made in the USA
Middletown, DE
15 August 2019